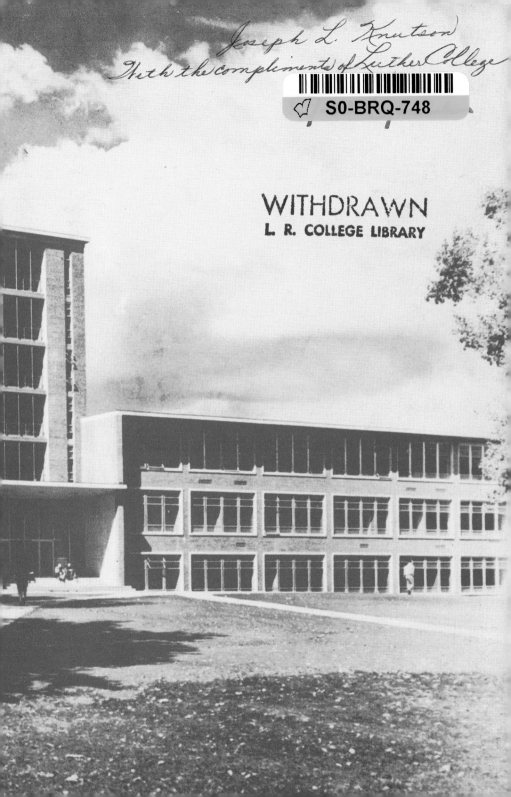

The
Mature
Luther

The
Mature
Luther

Theodore G. Tappert
Professor of Church History,
Lutheran Theological Seminary, Philadelphia, Pennsylvania

Willem J. Kooiman
Professor of Church History, University of Amsterdam, Holland

Lowell C. Green
Parish Pastor, Canby, Minnesota

LUTHER COLLEGE PRESS
DECORAH, IOWA

THE MATURE LUTHER

Martin Luther Lectures—Volume 3

© Luther College Press 1959

Library of Congress Catalog Card No. 57-9726

Manufactured in the United States of America

Introduction

Here for the third time, as St. Paul once remarked to the Christians in Corinth, we are coming to you. We could go on to say with Paul, "This will not be a burden," because we know you will enjoy reading, as we at Luther College enjoyed hearing, these lectures on various aspects of *The Mature Luther.* We hope the reader will accept Volume III of the Luther Lectures with the same critical approval that has been granted the earlier volumes, *Luther Today* and *More About Luther.*

We need not exert ourselves, I believe, to justify publications like this one. Even the enemies of the Gospel and antagonists of the heroes of Christian faith concede that the power generated by Martin Luther is still abroad in the world and is not diminishing. "While Luther has been dead for more than four centuries," writes one of the authors of this book, "he still speaks out with a certainty and a clarity which are of great help to us of the twentieth century." Some would question the word "help"; no one could question the certainty or clarity with which Luther speaks. Evangelical Lutherans and their colleges

37164

admit only one infallible speaker of truth: the Holy Spirit through and in the holy Word. We affirm also that Luther is one through whom the Lord has hitherto helped us, and that no more sure interpreter of the Gospel has been given to humanity than the Augustinian monk who cut his way through the religious accretions of centuries to rediscover the Good News.

We have in this series of lectures quite deliberately moved into the area of the biographical, in some respects even the popular and practical. Yet sound scholarship has not been sacrificed. In the hands of such skilled workmen as Theodore Tappert, Willem Kooiman, and Lowell Green, the later years of Martin Luther have been opened to us with loving yet critical care.

As the Martin Luther Lectures Committee reflected upon the areas which the 1958 Lectures might explore, a number of considerations suggested themselves. It was desirable, in the first place, to remember that the audience to which we owed the most was our own student body. To offer our students a healthy combination of theological and historical analysis and down-to-earth religious practicality became our first criterion. We were anxious, secondly, to present to our guests, including teachers, pastors, and theological students, a course of lectures which might stimulate a desire for more complete and accurate knowledge of him whose name we bear as Lutherans. In the third place, we wanted to produce, through the nine lectures, a book which might say something both new and timely. And in view of the emphasis in recent decades upon "the young Luther," we determined that "the mature Luther" should once again be scrutinized.

The most casual reading of Dr. Tappert's *Luther's Letters of Spiritual Counsel*—if one can be casual in reading so revealing and moving a collection of letters—is enough to indicate that no one in our day is better qualified to speak about Luther in his academic role than Dr. Tappert. In his lectures the biographical, the historical, and the theological are skillfully blended. Colorful anecdotes and quotations are employed, yet not as an end in themselves.

Representing European scholarship, and following in the train of E. Gordon Rupp and Regin Prenter who were Luther Lecturers in previous years, came the engaging and provocative Dutch historian Willem J. Kooiman, professor in the University of Amsterdam. Dr. Kooiman is well known to Americans because of his earlier visits to our country, his contributions to the work of the Lutheran World Federation during the past years, and his biography of Luther, *By Faith Alone*. Readers will miss an experience which the hearers had, because to have Dr. Kooiman behind the lectern is to have Martin Luther *redivivus:* alternately bold and gentle, hearty and sensitive, *forte* and *pianissimo* in volume, unyielding in principle yet broad in spirit. Something of these contrasts shows through even on the printed page. The reader is asked to pay particular attention to the essay entitled "Luther as He Saw Himself." Dr. Kooiman agreed with his hearers that exploring the self-consciousness of the volatile Dr. Luther was a demanding and yet fascinating task.

The final trio of lectures is clear evidence that one need not search the world over to find capable scholars of the Reformation period. Drawing upon materials assembled for his doctoral dissertation presented to the University of Erlangen, the midwestern parish pastor Lowell C. Green shows his concern for modern churchmanship and relevant theological scholarship as he speaks

of the relation between Luther and Philip Melanchthon. Dr. Green's second lecture is a balanced treatment of the contributions which Melanchthon made to
Luther, and is based on thorough knowledge of both
the sources and the secondary literature. The concluding
lecture of this volume contains an appraisal of the status
of Lutheran theological study in the United States.

To these gentlemen we are deeply grateful, not only
for their contribution to òur academic year at Luther
College, but for their personal graciousness during a
memorable four days. The presence of their respective
Katharinas enhanced those days.

We must acknowledge for the third time the interest
and considerable financial support of the Lutheran Broth-
erhood Life Insurance Society. To Chairman of the Board
J. A. O. Preus and President Carl F. Granrud go our
particular thanks for their continuing interest in the
Martin Luther Lecture Series. Gratitude is also hereby
expressed to the manager and the staff of Augsburg
Publishing House. The patience of George Nordwall,
Paul Martinsen, and William Gentz is equalled only by
their unfailing good humor. Professors John Bale and
Oivind Hovde of our College shared the pleasant edi-
torial labors.

In this, the ninety-eighth year of a College of the
Church, we submit to our wider constituency a volume
which we believe is a small but worthy contribution to
the knowing and the doing of truth. "Soli deo gloria,"
we pray, and we pray in the Savior's holy Name.

GERHARD L. BELGUM, *Chairman*
Division of Religion and Philosophy

Luther College
Fourth Monday in Lent, 1959

Contents

Theodore G. Tappert

Luther in His Academic Role

The Professor and His Students

The Theologian and the Study of History

The Professor of Theology

The Professor and His Students

THE formality of being registered as a student in the University of Wittenberg was uncomplicated. Prospective students simply sought out the rector, inscribed their names on the roll, and promised to obey the regulations.[1] However, reception into the academic community also involved a special ceremony of initiation, called "deposition," which older students inherited from the Middle Ages. It undoubtedly had its origin in the universal instinct among young men for horseplay and in their fondness for lording it over their juniors. The practice, which first arose among students, was countenanced, if not adopted, by authorities of medieval universities in an attempt, it appears, to keep it within reasonable bounds, and faculty members participated on invitation. The fledglings were called "yellow-bills" *(bejani)* who needed to be tamed before they could become acceptable members of the community.[2] After they had submitted to humiliating

---

[1] K. G. Bretschneider, *Corpus Reformatorum* (Halle, 1834), x. 993. Hereafter cited as "CR."

[2] Cf. Hastings Rashdall, *The Universities of Europe in the Middle Ages,* edited by F. M. Powicke and A. B. Emden (Oxford, 1936), Vol. III, pp. 376-385.

3

harassments, horns which had previously been attached to the students' heads were removed, salt was sprinkled on them in token of their need to be preserved from corruption, wine was poured on their heads to mark their entrance upon a new and more exalted kind of life, and finally they were "absolved," as it was called, from their former low estate and declared worthy of becoming students.[3]

Luther was invited to such ceremonies and sometimes participated in them. On one of the occasions when he addressed entering students at the formal conclusion of their initiation, he is reported to have said with that mingling of humor and earnestness which was so characteristic of his relations with his students: ("This ceremony is intended to make you humble, so that you may not be haughty and arrogant and given to wickedness) Such vices are monsters with horns, and these are not becoming to men or students. Therefore, humble yourselves. Learn to be patient. You will be subjected to molestations all your life. When you hold important offices in the future, burghers, peasants, noblemen, and your wives will harass you in various ways. When this happens, do not become impatient. Bear your cross and your troubles with equanimity and without murmuring. Remember that you were initiated into trouble in Wittenberg. Say that you first began to be 'hazed' in Wittenberg when you were a young man. Now that you are more distinguished, say that you have more grievous vexations to bear. So this your 'deposition' is only a symbol of human life in its troubles and castigations."[4] It need hardly be said that such initiations of students could easily get out of hand. By the seventeenth century, in fact, they descended to the level of a systematic

[3]CR x, 97, 98.

[4]WA TR iv, 4714 (1539). Cf. also WA xlviii, 709, 710; WA TR iv, 5024 (1540); WA TR vi, 7033 (undated).

and brutal exploitation of younger students which was suppressed only with difficulty.

In his earlier years Luther complained that the universities were "places for training young people in Greek glory in which loose living prevails."[5] In spite of, and to some extent because of, the monastic atmosphere which dominated the universities at the close of the Middle Ages, the want of refinement which was characteristic of society in general affected the conduct of students. We must not allow romantic notions of the Reformation to obscure the fact that much of this coarseness of life continued throughout the sixteenth century. Besides, there was a tendency then, as now, for students to abuse their freedom from parental oversight. The statutes of the University of Wittenberg especially deplored "the folly of many who think that when they are sent to college they are liberated from domestic discipline."[6] The Reformers were not disposed to believe that behavior could be improved by merely imposing a multitude of laws. "We learn from experience, history, and also Holy Scripture," Luther once put it, "that the less law there is, the more justice, and the fewer commands there are, the more good works."[7] In similar vein the university statutes asserted, "We do not set up laws other than those which God Himself left us" in the Ten Commandments.[8] Nevertheless, some regulation of individual and common life was necessary.

The earlier monastic contempt for the body which had led to the discouragement of physical exercise and the prohibition of "profane games" was no longer in evidence.[9] On the contrary, Luther often advocated "manly bodily

[5]WA vi, 457 (Address to the Christian Nobility, 1520).
[6]CR x, 995.
[7]WA vi, 353 (Treatise on the New Testament, 1520).
[8]CR x, 995.
[9]Cf. Rashdall, op. cit., III, pp. 419-427.

5

exercises," positively for their salutary effect on health and negatively for their value in counteracting soft and licentious living.[10] Students were accustomed to playing ball in the square in front of the castle gate, and they engaged in fencing.[11] They also went swimming in the Elbe River.[12]

The university statutes permitted students to attend occasional dances "for the sake of honest discipline" and because they could there "learn reverence and modesty in conversation and deportment." The statutes guarded against abuses by adding, "We shall severely punish those who foolishly cause disturbance at such gatherings, and especially those who are immodest in their dancing and lead girls in gyrations [in gyrum ducunt] beyond the common harmony of modest dancing."[13] Luther approved, for he said, "When young fellows and girls engage in round dances and carry on with decent music and movements, it is an urbane exercise [officium humanitatis] which pleases me very much."[14] In a sermon addressed to students as well as townspeople Luther asked, "Is it a sin to pipe and dance at a wedding inasmuch as it is said that many sins come from dancing?" He answered his own question by saying: "I do not know if there were dances among the Jews. But since it is a custom in our land—like dressing up, eating, drinking, and being merry—I cannot condemn it except when it is excessive, indecent, or immoderate. That sin has been connected with it is not alone the fault of dancing, for sin is also committed at table and in church. Eating and drinking are not to blame if some become pigs at it. Where dancing is engaged in

---

[10]Cf. WA TR iii, 3470 (1536).
[11]Walter Friedensburg, ed., *Urkundenbuch der Universität Wittenberg* (Magdeburg, 1926), Vol. I, p. 228 (1543), p. 244 (1545).
[12]WA xxix, 401 (Sermon, 1529).
[13]CR x, 997.
[14]WA TR ii, 1434 (1532)

6

decently, let the custom prevail at weddings. Go ahead and dance! (Faith and love are lost neither by dancing nor by sitting out the dance, provided you do what you do with decency and moderation.)[15] Older people, Luther suggested another time, ought to attend dances to watch over the young people.[16] Philip Melanchthon not only watched over the young people but participated, for Urban Balduin wrote to a friend from Wittenberg, "I saw Melanchthon dance with the dean's wife, and it was marvelous to behold."[17] It is hardly surprising that the liberty granted to students was abused by some. During his term as rector of the university Philip Melanchthon posted this notice: "To the Students: We understand that at public dances some allow themselves the liberty of certain silly behavior, which is not proper and at the same time affords danger to the girls who are dancing. Besides, since dances ought not to be a barbaric or disgraceful pastime but were introduced for the sake of discipline in order that young men might learn to show honest attention to the female sex, dances have a good purpose. Accordingly it is not to be allowed that a custom which was introduced for discipline and refinement [humanitas] should be spoiled by indecency and buffoonery. We therefore forbid leading girls about in gyrations while dancing, as has been done by some. We also forbid other improper kinds of dancing. . . . We ask you to remember that a school is a laboratory of virtues, and in a Christian school we ought especially to excel in piety, lest evil examples

---

[15]WA xvii, II, 64 (Sermon, 1525). Cf. WA xxxiv, II, 214 (Sermon, 1531).

[16]WA xxxii, 209 (Sermon, 1530).

[17]Georg Buchwald, ed., *Zur Wittenberger Stadt- und Universitäts-Geschichte: Briefe aus Wittenberg an M. Stephan Roth* (Leipzig, 1893), p. 62 (1529). The "dean's wife" was the wife of the dean of the theological faculty, the Rev. John Bugenhagen.

give the teaching of religion a bad report. We therefore command that in your whole manner of living you act modestly and quietly."[18]

Other occasions for amusement and distraction were readily found. Familiar is the participation of the students in Luther's burning of the papal bull of excommunication and of books of canon law and scholastic theology in 1520. This was the notice, posted on the bulletin board, which brought out the students: "Whoever you are who are zealous for evangelical truth, come to the Chapel of the Holy Cross beyond the walls of our town about the ninth hour. There, according to ancient and even apostolic precedent [cf. Acts 19:19], the impious books of papal constitutions and scholastic theology will be burned. . . . Come on, pious and studious youth! Attend this godly and religious spectacle!"[19] The students responded with alacrity and followed the brief act of Luther's defiance with a celebration of their own. The following spring, Luther reported in a letter, the students "carried about a mock pope in ludicrous and lofty pomp. Finally, acting as if they intended to throw him into the fountain in the market-place, they chased the pope and his cardinals, bishops, and chamberlains into the various quarters of the town according to a very funny and well-conceived plan. Christ's enemy, who mocks the greatest kings and even Christ Himself, deserved in this way to be made a laughing-stock."[20] It is obvious that Luther enjoyed this act, which took place during the traditional pre-Lenten carnival season.

Later on Luther frowned on the observance of Lenten fasts and the *Fastnacht* or Mardi gras which preceded them. Students were admonished by Luther in a sermon

---

[18]CR x, 79-81 (between 1530 and 1539).
[19]WA vii, 183 (prepared by Philip Melanchthon).
[20]WA Br ii, 266 (Feb. 17, 1521).

not to engage in the customary mummeries,[21] and he would not admit masquerading students to his home. A few of them determined to outfox their professor. Dressing themselves as miners, slate-cutters, and ore-breakers, they went to the home of Luther (who was himself a miner's son) with a chess set. When Luther was informed that some miners were at the door, he called out, "Let them in. They are my countrymen and swing their axes as my dear father used to. Because they spend the whole week underground in the dampness and bad air, they must be allowed to have some honest fun and recreation once in a while." The company sat down at Luther's table, set up the chess figures, and one of them engaged the Reformer, who appears to have been a skillful player, in a game. Luther checkmated his opponent, and all of them remained for some time afterwards to eat, drink, and sing with great merriment.[22] When in 1542 the carnival season was at hand, Luther felt that frivolity was especially out of place in view of the threatening danger of invasion by the Turks. From his sick-bed he sent out an admonition in which the students were addressed in this fashion: "A poor, old preacher, I beg you, my students, for God's sake to conduct yourselves quietly, decently, and respectably, attending to that for which you came here and for which your parents sent you here at great cost."[23]

Some students' pranks evoked a different response from Luther than those of the chess-playing masqueraders. During the disturbances caused in Wittenberg by Andrew Carlstadt and the "Zwickau prophets" while Luther was still in Wartburg Castle in 1521 and 1522, some students

---

[21]WA xlvii, 665, 666 (Sermon, 1539). Cf. Friedensburg, *op. cit.*, I, p. 223 (1540).

[22]Johann Mathesius, *Mathesius Predigten über Luthers Leben.* Hrsg. von Georg Buchwald (Stuttgart, 1904), p. 240-242.

[23]WA liii, 211, 212 (1542).

prevented the priests in the parish church from saying Mass by pelting them with stones, and later they carried off the missals and drove the priests from the altar. In an adjoining village other students interrupted a sermon by shouting, "Dear people, this man lies and expounds Holy Scriptures wrongly."[24] Luther rebuked such offensive conduct, and in another somewhat similar situation he said, "Our Lord God should not be molested in His servants."[25]

There were times when Luther was himself the object of attack. Among his students were many who "considered themselves exceedingly fortunate" to live in a time when they could know and study under him.[26] On the other hand, there were some who felt like the student who was reported to have said, after hearing the Reformer preach for the first time, that if Luther preached that way again he would take up a stone and hit him on the head with it in the church.[27] Luther himself could say, "I maintain that there are many wicked knaves and spies here who listen to us and rejoice when scandal and disunity arise."[28] In 1538 a student named Simon Lemnius put a slim volume of verses on sale before the church doors in Wittenberg. A copy fell into Luther's hands, and seeing in it a veiled attack on prominent persons in Wittenberg and a defense of foes of the Reformation, he took steps to have further circulation of the booklet stopped. On the following Sunday, after his sermon, Luther made a statement about the affair to the congregation.[29] About a year later

[24]Hermann Barge, *Andreas Bodenstein von Karlstadt*, 2 vols. (Leipzig, 1905), I, pp. 342, 417.

[25]WA TR vi, 6794 (undated).

[26]See the letter of Felix Ulscenius to Wolfgang Capito, Jan. 13, 1521, in Martin Luther, *Luther's Correspondence and Other Contemporary Letters*, tr. and ed. by Preserved Smith (Philadelphia, 1913), Vol. I, pp. 439, 440.

[27]Friedensburg, *op. cit.*, I, p. 103.

[28]WA TR iv, 5126 (1540).

[29]WA 1, 350, 351 (Declaration against Simon Lemnius, 1538).

it was reported that an English student of law in Wittenberg, who gave himself out to be an Italian, wrote a lampoon in which Luther and Melanchthon were pilloried. Among other things, he wrote that Luther related old wives' tales in his sermons and that, although Luther was a man of little learning, all the students hung on his every word.[30] Here we find an indirect testimony to the popularity of Luther and the high esteem in which he was generally held. Beyond this, the attacks throw light not only on the inclination of students to engage in pranks but also on the bitter feeling engendered by the Reformation movement.

Students were also involved in the "town and gown" battles which had a long and violent history reaching back before the foundation of Wittenberg University. Friction and conflict between townspeople and the university community resulted in part from the special privileges and status which academic persons traditionally enjoyed and in part from the belief, sometimes real and sometimes imagined, that the one group was taking advantage of the other. In a small town like Wittenberg contacts between students and townspeople were especially close, and the fact that many students were housed in private homes rather than in college dormitories increased the possibilities of friction. The rector of the university once posted a notice to warn students against bespattering passers-by in the streets by emptying their chamber pots on them from their windows. (Interesting light is shed on the crudity of the age by the rector's suggestion that students should look about before dumping the contents of their slop buckets on the streets; the emptying of the buckets on the

---

[30]Georg Buchwald, ed., "Lutherana," in *Archiv für Reformationsgeschichte*, XXV (1928), p. 66.

street was not prohibited.)[31] Whether this warning was a consequence of malicious acts of students against towns-people is not apparent. But the existence of violent out-breaks of hostility can easily be documented.

In 1520 several town and gown riots occurred, and Lu-ther introduced the subject into his sermons. "Some," he reported later, "said that I favored the students too much, and some the contrary."[32] The university statutes tried to curb the students. "Since it is necessary to preserve the common peace of the town," they provided, "we shall severely punish all authors of tumults, vagabonds by day or night, rioters, assemblers of mobs, those who storm buildings, thieves, cheats, ravagers of gardens, and such as in any way spitefully do harm to others or cause them loss."[33] This catalog of offenses was obviously based on concrete experiences with student behavior. Little change resulted from the statutes, which were read annually to the students. Curfews were intended to keep students off the streets at night, and in a further attempt at restraint, students were forbidden to carry such weapons as swords, knives, daggers, crossbows, and lead bullets within the town limits. Enforcement of this regulation proved dif-ficult because danger to travelers demanded that students be armed whenever they went beyond the walls of the town. Moreover, it was observed in 1538, "How the stu-dents are to be prohibited we do not know, for they cannot go about without a bread knife, as they say"[34]—a realistic observation at a time when students carried their eating utensils about with them.

[31]Gustav Kawerau, "Aus dem Wittenberger Universitätsleven," in *Archiv für Reformationsgeschichte*, XVII (1920), p. 8.

[32]WA Br ii, 49, 142, 143, 144, 145, 163, 164 (Luther to George Spalatin, Feb. 24, July 14 and 17, Aug. 5, 1520).

[33]CR x, 996.

[34]CR x, 998; Friedensburg, *op. cit.*, I, pp. 96, 97.

In a sermon in 1538 Luther complained that the devil "is now trying to cause friction between the artisans [of the town] and the students. . . . He must at times have a wicked knave or two to lead a crowd astray." "Do not play along with such knaves," Luther warned.[35] In 1543 a conflict occurred between some fishermen and some students. It was difficult for the town and university authorities to get at the facts. One student said that the fracas began when he was attacked by a young fisherman, was struck by a stone which injured his eye, and had his coat stolen. Another student said that when he rebuked a boy for cursing his mother, a group of fishermen jumped him and one of them stabbed him. Still another student complained that when he was walking by the house of a barber the contents of a chamber pot were spattered over him, and this led to outcries and threats. A burgher reported that a stone broke a window in his house and injured his eye.[36] Perhaps all of these things happened and were parts of the same battle. Among other reasons for the hostility between students and townspeople was the conviction of many students that they were being fleeced, and Luther charged that in order to make more money merchants and tavern keepers induced students to spend beyond their means.[37] He berated merchants for selling shoddy wares, brewers for adulterating beer with ashes and thus endangering health, farmers for withholding their produce to create an artificial shortage and raise prices.[38] When a student spent the 200 gulden he got from home without paying his board bill, it was recommended that henceforth parents should not entrust large sums of money to their sons but should

---

[35]WA xlvi, 156-161 (Sermon, 1538).

[36]Friedensburg, op. cit., I, pp. 227-234; Kawerau, op. cit., p. 5.

[37]WA xli, 471 (Sermon, 1535).

[38]WA xxvii, 418, 419 (Sermon, 1528): WA xxxiv, II, 21 (Sermon, 1531); Friedensburg, op. cit., I, p. 240 (1544).

rather send it to some friend who might see to it that bills for necessities were paid.[39]

Contacts between students and townspeople were also of another sort. "We have a large number of young men from a variety of lands," Luther wrote to the elector of Saxony, "and the girls [in town] have become bold, run after the fellows in their rooms and wherever else they can, and offer them their love gratis. I hear that many parents have called their sons home and say, 'We send you our sons to study and you hang wives on their necks and alienate them from us.' The result is that this school gets a bad reputation."[40] In this letter Luther was deploring secret engagements; he was not suggesting that university students cease associating with girls. In a lecture to the students Luther once had occasion to refer to the monks who tried to remain chaste by fleeing from the sight of women. "To avoid seeing women," he said, "is not a true remedy against lust, nor do you cure vices by abstention but by control and proper use."[41] While Luther was far from prohibiting "dates" with girls, he maintained that serious students would not spend all their time chasing after them.[42] When an able student once became ill, Luther dealt with him in a very friendly way, waited until he recovered, and then said to him, "The reason for your illness is love. Studying seldom has this effect!"[43] Luther's understanding for this side of his students' lives is reflected in his correspondence concerning a twenty-year-old student named John Schneidewein who had fallen in love with a girl from Wittenberg and desired to marry her. Luther urged the reluctant mother to consent to the

[39]*Ibid.*, I, pp. 197, 198 (1538).
[40]WA Br x, 500, 501 (Jan. 22, 1544).
[41]WA xlii, 496 (Lectures on Genesis, 1535-45).
[42]WA TR vi, 6929 (undated).
[43]WA TR iii, 2894 (1538).

engagement and marriage when he wrote to her: "Your son John is attached by a great love to an honorable girl here. . . . I am unwilling to see his hope turn to ashes. The girl pleases him very much, her station in life is not unlike his, and she is, besides, a pious girl of an honorable family. . . . It therefore behooves you, as a loving mother, to give your consent."[44]

Here, too, there were some students who, "when liberated from papal tyranny by the Gospel, abused Christian liberty."[45] From time to time Wittenberg, like other university towns, was invaded by women with a less savory reputation who enticed some students away from the town girls. In 1522 three women were driven out of Wittenberg on account of their loose morals.[46] The problem still existed sixteen years later when Luther declared in a sermon: "I hear that some of those students are saying that they no longer wish to study here but prefer to chase after whores. . . . Women are to be held in honor until they bring shame on themselves."[47] Five years after this Luther became aware that some students were frequenting a wooded area outside of town where some prostitutes had set themselves up in business. He posted a warning to the students which reads in part: "As an old and faithful preacher I ask you in fatherly fashion, dear children, that you believe assuredly that the evil spirit sent these whores here and that they are dreadful, shabby, stinking, loathsome, and syphilitic, as daily experience unfortunately demonstrates. Let every good student warn his fellows.

[44]WA Br viii, 453-455 (Luther to Ursula Schneidewein, June 4, 1539). Translation from T. G. Tappert, *Luther: Letters of Spiritual Counsel* (Philadelphia, 1955), pp. 287, 288. Cf. WA Br viii, 492, 493 (Luther to Ursula Schneidewein, July 10, 1539).

[45]Mathesius, *op. cit.*, p. 147.

[46]Preserved Smith and Charles M. Jacobs, eds., *Luther's Correspondence and Other Contemporary Letters*, Vol. II (Philadelphia, 1918), p. 131 (Felix Ulscenius to Wolfgang Capito, July 20, 1522).

[47]WA xlvi, 156-161 (Sermon, 1538).

Such a syphilitic whore can give her disease to ten, twenty, thirty, and more good people, and so she is to be accounted a murderess, as worse than a poisoner. . . . I must speak plainly. . . . You foolish young men think that you must not suffer, that as soon as you feel ardent a whore must be found to satisfy you. . . . But it is not necessary to indulge your every passion at once. . . . The judgment of God stands: 'Neither let us commit fornication, as some of them committed' [I. Cor. 10:8.]"[48] From the tender and sympathetic treatment of students who were in love Luther turned here to unleash thunderbolts of wrath against those who succumbed to immorality in one of its worse forms.

So misbehavior of students ran the gamut from making unnecessary noise and quarreling to street brawling, tavern crawling, rioting with townspeople, and commerce with prostitutes. The presence in the student body of young men of different national and cultural backgrounds, all of whom were cut loose from home ties, accentuated the problem of discipline. "It is truly a gift of God," the university authorities once reported to the elector in commenting on the diversity of students, "that the disturbance is not greater."[49] Luther threatened to send home the students who were guilty of serious infractions of the university statutes,[50] and some were actually sent packing. The Reformer realized, as he put it, that "what happens in secret I cannot judge, and it is altogether possible that I do not hear of everything."[51] But he was persuaded that infractions and disturbances had to be ascribed to a small minority. "We have a fine, quiet school, but a few of the

---

[48]WA TR iv, 4857n (1543). Translation from Tappert, *op. cit.*, pp. 292-294. Cf. WA Br x, 333, 334 (Luther to Justus Jonas, June 18, 1543).

[49]Friedensburg, *op. cit.*, I, p. 239 (1544).

[50]WA xli, 471, 472 (Sermon, 1535).

[51]WA Br vii, 423 (Luther to Margrave George of Brandenburg, May 29, 1536).

students are black sheep."[52] It needs to be observed in this connection that, then as now, departures from the normal pattern of life were singled out and recorded while adherence to the accepted proprieties was taken for granted. One must therefore be careful not to generalize and exaggerate.

The same may be said about the application of students to their studies. The sigh of Luther, "Would that our young men studied more diligently and applied themselves to theology!"[53] may be taken as the hopeful, yet despairing, wish of all teachers everywhere. This is not to say that there were not concrete instances of sloth. Luther had occasion to complain that, despite great advantages and opportunities, some had no zeal for study and were lazy and negligent. At his table he once read young Hans von Auerswald a lecture on his want of application even though he had a good head, the gifts for study, and parents who were spending a good deal on him and were eager to have him learn something. When he showed no signs of reform, Luther said to him: "I shall not hear of this, nor shall I suffer such an example of disobedience in my house and at my table, even if you possessed the wealth of a count. Pay heed to what I say, for I shall not stand for such conduct from you or from anybody else!"[54]

In 1527 and 1536 the town of Wittenberg was so seriously threatened with the plague that the university was temporarily removed to Jena. At other times, too, the fear of epidemic disease gave some students an excuse to interrupt their studies. "I have observed," Luther wrote to the elector on such an occasion with thinly veiled humor, "that many of the young students have rejoiced over rumors of

---

[52]WA xlvi, 178 (Sermon, 1538). Cf. Friedensburg, *op. cit.*, I, p. 247 (1545).
[53]WA TR iii, 3872 (1538).
[54]WA TR vi, 7032 (1539).

pestilence, for some of them have developed sores from carrying their schoolbags, some have acquired colic from their books, some have developed scabs on the fingers with which they write, some have picked up goutiness from their papers, and many have found their ink to be getting moldy. In addition, they have devoured letters from their mothers, and these have made them heartsick and homesick."[55] When death overtook a student, whether as a result of the plague or from some other cause, Luther took it upon himself to write a letter of comfort to the mourning parents.[56]

The personal interest in the welfare of his students which was suggested in such letters also manifested itself in the readiness with which Luther interceded in behalf of needy students. "There are many godly and gifted students." Luther reported, "who live all year on bread and water and endure frost and cold in order that they may study the Holy Scriptures and the Word of God."[57] With a student from Poland especially in mind, Luther wrote, "Many who come here from all lands are poor, and we cannot take care of all of them because we have nothing left."[58] The rising cost of living made the situation even more desperate. "Many students," Luther observed, "are forced to leave on account of the wickedness of those who are withholding grain" in an attempt to push up prices.[59] Under such circumstances Luther wrote to kings, princes, town councils, and private persons who had means in an attempt to secure financial help for particular students in need. For example, to the duke of Mecklenburg he wrote: "Matthew Roloff, a fellow-countryman of yours from

[55]WA Br vii, 207, 208 (Luther to Elector John Frederick, July 9, 1535). Translation from Tappert, *op. cit.*, p. 246.
[56]For some examples see *ibid.*, pp. 61, 64, 72, 78 (1531-1544).
[57]WA Br vii, 61 (Luther to Dorothy Joerger, Apr. 27, 1534).
[58]WA Br viii, 423, 424 (Luther to Sixtus Oelhofen, Apr. 29, 1539).
[59]WA Br viii, 397 (Luther to Melanchthon, Mar. 26, 1539).

18

Quassow, asked me to write to you after he has been here for a while as a student and has given signs of promise, ... with the request that you graciously support him for several years with the income from a vacated fief or with a stipend. Without it he cannot remain here for any length of time and must abandon his studies on account of poverty. This would be a pity since he has come from such a distance."[60] A widow in Wittenberg willed her house and property to provide scholarship aid to a student,[61] and another widow gave a gift of 500 gulden with the stipulation that the interest from the invested sum should be used for the support of two students annually.[62] The elector of Saxony established forty scholarships, and later forty-five additional ones, for poor students from his territory and stipulated that they be examined in their studies annually in order to demonstrate that they were deserving of support.[63] Although some students who received stipends were negligent in their studies, Luther believed that, on the whole, the poorest young men made the best students, for "aristocratic fellows who carry heavy purses and provisions do not study."[64]

In his relations with his students Luther could be stern and severe, as we have seen, but he was generally remembered by his students as friendly and sympathetic. Some, like the sensitive Jerome Weller, did not feel entirely at ease in the presence of the awesome, learned, and sometimes blustering Reformer. But most of his students appear to have been attracted by the unaffected openness, the thoughtfulness, and the genuineness which were apparent behind his rough outward manner. A little incident will

---

[60]WA Br vii, 593 (Luther to Duke of Mecklenburg, Nov. 18, 1536).
[61]WA TR v, 6302 (undated).
[62]WA Br vi, 273-275, 407-410, 461, 462, 546, 547.
[63]CR x, 1013. Cf. Friedensburg op. cit., I, pp. 186, 250, 254.
[64]WA TR iii, 3599 (1537). Cf. WA TR, vi, 7050 (undated).

serve to illustrate this. In his later years Luther often found it difficult to sit still for an extended period of time because of his age and the pains which racked his body. One Sunday, when he sat in church listening to his good friend and colleague John Bugenhagen preach, he felt restless and could not sit through the long sermon. He quietly slipped out of the church, and "many students left with him and escorted him to his home."[65] This was a simple act which revealed the affection and the respect of the students for their aging professor.

[65] Mathäus Ratzeberger, *Die handschriftliche Geschichte Ratzebergers über Luther und seine Zeit,* hrsg. von d. Chr. Gotth. Neudecker (Jena, 1850), p. 88.

The Theologian and the Study of History

IT IS the task of the historian to assemble, analyze, and correlate evidence and on the basis of such evidence to reconstruct some part of the past into a record which is faithful to what actually happened. Every honest historian knows that he can achieve this goal only within limits. In his desire to find more meaning than his evidence warrants, he may look for help from those non-historians as well as historians whose speculations have suggested a variety of patterns or laws of history—cyclical, spiral, evolutionary, progressive, regressive, biological, cataclysmic, causal. Unhappily, such theories of history do not fit the known data. The past is punctuated by the unexpected, the unpredictable, the unique, the unaccountable. A historian would distort the past if he imposed a neat pattern of regularity on the irregularities of history, for in spite of the popular saying, history does not repeat itself.

Although the professional historian must dismiss most of the old theories of history as unserviceable and as more of a hindrance than a help to him in his craft, he should nevertheless be grateful for some contributions which the philosophy of history has made. If it has done nothing else, it has served to remind the historian that he must be conscious of his own presuppositions and that he, too, must be concerned with the meaning of human life and the relation of man to the totality of existence. For the Christian historian this would of necessity imply that any interpretation of history must take God into account. It is at this point that we may well inquire whether Martin Luther has any help to offer the historian.[1]

At the outset it should be said that Luther was not what we should call a professional historian. He made history, but he wrote nothing that we should call either a history or a philosophy of history. Yet he had a keen interest in history and the work of historians, an interest which grew with the years and led him in his maturer years to write prefaces for the historical studies of other men. ("Historians," he wrote in one of these prefaces, "are the most useful people and the best teachers, and they cannot be sufficiently honored, praised, and thanked."[2]) Luther himself made diligent use of the histories and chronicles which were accessible to him. They provided him with some of the weapons with which he attacked the authority of popes and councils. They enabled him to understand that the

---

[1] Growing interest in the philosophy and theology of history is reflected in the following studies, listed chronologically, which treat Luther from a variety of angles: Ernst Schaefer, *Luther als Kirchenhistoriker* (Gütersloh, 1897); Walther Koehler, *Luther und die Kirchengechichte* (Erlangen, 1900); Karl Bauer, *Die Wittenberger Universitätstheologie und die Aufänge der Reformation* (Tübingen, 1928); Hanns Lilje, *Luthers Geschichtsanschauung* (Berlin, 1932); Erich Kohlmeyer, "Die Geschichtsbetrachtung Luthers," in *Archiv für Reformationsgeschichte*, XXXVII (1940), pp. 150-170; Heinz Zahrnt, *Luther deutet Geschichte: Erfolg und Misserfolg* (Munich, 1952); Hans Walter Krumwiede, *Glaube und Geschichte in der Theologie Luthers* (Göttingen, 1952); Gunnar Hillerdal, "Prophetische Züge in Luthers Geschichtsdeutung," in *Studia Theologica*, VII, 2 (Lund, 1954), pp. 105-124. My purpose here is more modest: to suggest a theological justification for the work of the historian.

[2] WA 1, 384 (Preface to Capella's History, 1538).

22

church had not always been the same, that in the course of the centuries there had been significant and sometimes fateful changes in the teaching and worship as well as the organization of the church.

The tools for such insights had been furnished by the Renaissance, and the humanists also taught Luther the importance of sources and the critical use of them. He rejected legends and challenged the genuineness of some writings traditionally ascribed to such men as Augustine and Ambrose. He was unwilling to believe that there was a man named Aesop who wrote Aesop's Fables and maintained, instead, that they were edited in their present form by somebody who had collected the fables of earlier wise men. He doubted the genuineness of some of the superscriptions to the Psalms, and he frequently insisted that the Bible should be interpreted in its historical context. In his later life he declared: "I found it very difficult to give up my long indulgence in allegorizing. Nevertheless, I recognized that allegories were foolish speculations and, as it were, the scum of Holy Scripture! It is the historical sense of Scripture that alone teaches truly and solidly. After this has been treated and properly understood, allegories may be used as adornments and decorations by which the history may be illustrated or depicted. . . . Like oratory, allegory should only adorn history; it is worthless to prove anything."[3] In all of this Luther may be said to have been a child of his time who made use of the new learning of the Renaissance. But he went beyond his contemporaries when he probed into the deeper meaning of history and related it to his theology.

X (Luther took the reality of God very seriously) God was for him the ultimate reality, more real even than the visible things of this earth. God is present everywhere,

---

[3]WA xlii, 173, 174 (Lectures on Genesis, 1535-45).

even in a rustling leaf.[4] "The world is full of God, and He fills it all without being bound or limited by it, for He is at the same time outside and above all creatures."[5] This omnipresent God who is at once immanent and transcendent is an active God. "He would be . . . a ridiculous God if He could not and did not do all things or if anything could be done without Him. . . . We were not made by ourselves, we do not live by ourselves, we do not do anything by ourselves, but by God's omnipotence."[6] That God must be the almighty doer of all things is known, however obscurely, by all men, whether non-Christian or Christian.[7]

Such a description of God's power and activity in history introduces problems. For one thing, if God does all things, how can we account for the apparent inequities and contradictions in history? The whole course of history shows that again and again the wicked prosper while the righteous suffer.[8] How can this be if God is sovereign and governs all things? Good men die while evil men live.[9] Sometimes a man who works hard has little to show for it while another man who takes it easy grows rich. The worst knaves have the best kingdoms.[10] Alexander the Great, the worst of men, ruled successfully over the Greeks, and Luther observed that in his time the cruel Turks were winning victory after victory.[11] "This," declared Luther, "is what always happens in all history. Where God acts, He presents Himself in such a foolish role that in the eyes of reason He falls to the ground."[12] That wicked men should

[4] WA xix, 226 (Prophet Jonah Expounded, 1526).
[5] WA xxiii, 135, 136 (That These Words Still Stand, 1527).
[6] WA xviii, 718 (Bondage of the Will, 1525).
[7] E.g., WA xviii, 618, 709 (Bondage of the Will, 1525).
[8] WA TR iii, 3234 (1532).
[9] WA TR i, 44 (1531).
[10] WA xxxii, 403, 471 (Sermons on Matthew, 1530-32).
[11] WA xlii, 509 (Lectures on Genesis, 1535-45).
[12] WA xxiv, 297 (Sermons on Genesis, 1527).

enjoy success is a grievous offense which tries the patience of saints and confounds philosophers and the wise of this world. Reason cannot solve the offense.[13]

Then there is another problem. If God does all things, what about such evils in the world as misfortune, calamity, famine, war, and death? Luther boldly asserted that God is behind these too. "God has death and all things in His hand. . . . Everywhere He is present—in death, in hell, among our enemies, even in their hearts. For He has made all things and so governs them that all things must do His will."[14] Luther went so far as to describe the course of history as God's jugglery, to picture the world as a chessboard on which God moves figures at His will, and to compare God's activity in history with a game which a parent plays with a child and in which an apple is given and taken away.[15] Such drastic figures as these were intended by Luther to affirm as strongly as possible that God is sovereign in history, that not even the evils of this life happen apart from God's will and activity.

Is God, then, the author of evil? "Reason," wrote Luther, "concedes that God works all in all and that without Him nothing happens or is done, for He is almighty, and this belongs to His omnipotence." Even Satan and wicked men "are subject to God's omnipotence and activity. Inasmuch as God works and does all in all, He necessarily acts in Satan and the wicked too. He works in them as He finds them, according to what they are. That is, since they are inclined away from God and are evil, and since they are mightily moved by the activity of God's omnipotence, they do only what is evil and opposed to God, just as a rider

[13]WA xlii, 509 (Lectures on Genesis, 1535-45); WA xl, III, 227 (Psalms of Degrees, 1532-33).
[14]WA xix, 219, 220 (Prophet Jonah Expounded, 1526).
[15]WA xix, 360 (Jonah, 1526); WA TR v, 6135; WA xliii, 230 (Genesis, 1535-45).

who rides a horse that is lame in one or two legs rides the horse as it is; in other words, the horse runs lamely. What can the rider do? He rides a lame horse just as he rides a sound horse. One is lame, another is not. He cannot do otherwise unless the horse is made sound." This does not mean that God does evil. Evil happens when God uses evil men who cannot escape being moved by God's power. "Hence it happens that the wicked man can never do anything but err and sin because divine power does not allow him to be idle but carries him along, and he must will, desire, and do according as he is. . . . The fault lies in the instruments, which God does not allow to remain idle. Thus evil occurs under God's impulse, just as a carpenter cuts badly with a dull and jagged ax."[16]

Here another question may be asked. If evil men can only do evil, why does God not suspend the activity of His omnipotence so as to stop the evil in the world? Luther's answer to this question was that even to ask it is to wish that God should cease to be God. Why God does not suspend His rule belongs ultimately to the mystery of God's majesty, which must remain incomprehensible to us.[17] Meanwhile Luther insisted tirelessly that it is the almighty God who acts in and rules over history. Things cannot therefore happen by chance or luck. They do not happen simply as a result of man's wit, wisdom, and power. Nor are they a consequence of mechanically operating laws of nature.[18] The living God is active in history.

All of this must raise a final, and for our purpose a crucial, question. If God acts in history and if we are to ascribe all things to His omnipotence, how is it possible for a historian to find any meaning in human history at all?

---

[16]WA xviii, 709 (Bondage of the Will, 1525).

[17]WA xviii, 712 (Bondage of the Will, 1525).

[18]E.g., WA xv, 370 (Psalm 127 Expounded for the Christians in Riga, 1524); WA xlii, 509, 354 (Lectures on Genesis, 1535-45).

How can a historian even presume to undertake the study of history? If God acts in everything that happens, one might expect either a monotonous uniformity in historical events or an equally shapeless capriciousness. We have already observed that the former is not what we find; instead of monotonous uniformity we find that history is marked by change, variety, irregularity, uniqueness, the unexpected and incalculable. Luther was fully aware of this.[19] Only canon lawyers, who were accustomed to reconcile contradictory things, might, Luther intimated, try to find harmony and uniformity where it does not in fact exist. Not even God's judgment is automatic, for if God were to strike with thunder and lightning whenever men sinned He would soon run out of thunder and lightning.[20] The other alternative would seem to be that God acts capriciously in history. If this is so, human history must remain formless and meaningless, a tale told by an idiot— at least as long as we look at it from a horizontal perspective, through the eyes of men. But even if we could look at history from a vertical perspective, as God sees it, it must be without purpose. And of course we cannot see it as God sees it, for His ways are not our ways and our thoughts are not His thoughts.

But the history of the world and of mankind is not to be described in either of these ways, Luther suggested. To be sure, God acts in history. It is not as if He created everything in the beginning and then let nature take its own independent course, for then God would be no more than a shoemaker or tailor.[21] God continues to work and act in the world.[22] We often fail to appreciate this because

---

[19]E.g., WA xxxii, 475, 510 (Sermons on Matthew, 1530-32).
[20]WA li, 263, 206 (Exposition of Psalm 101, 1534-35). Cf. WA TR v, No. 5189 (1540).
[21]WA xlvi, 560, 561 (Exposition of John, 1537-40).
[22]WA xviii, 747 (Bondage of the Will, 1525).

the works of creation which God continues to perform are commonplace in our eyes. We regard God's creation of Adam and Eve as incredible and do not recognize the amazing work of God's creation in the continuing propagation of the race. In this connection Luther quoted the pagan poet,

> Rare things will e'er delight our eyes
> But common things are no surprise.[23]

Among such miracles of God's continuing creation Luther mentions that the sun shines, that fire warms, that water furnishes fish, that the earth yields grain, that cows calve, that hens lay eggs. These are not small things simply because they happen every day.[24]

In all these instances, it is to be observed, God does not act directly; He acts mediately through His creatures. To be sure, God is able to act directly, but it does not please Him to deal with us face to face in this life.[25] "Although God could have created you and provided for you without parents," Luther once declared, "He wished that your father beget you and that your mother nurse you. So in our everyday life necessary works should be done, fields should be plowed, planted, harvested, etc. Afterwards God will do what pleases Him. But if you should say, 'I shall not give my child milk because if he is destined to live he will live,' you will make a mistake and sin gravely. God gave mothers breasts to feed their offspring. He could indeed feed the child without milk, but He does not wish to."[26] In another context Luther said that "God could rule the world without judges and civil authorities. He could hang a thief and protect a good man without burgomas-

---

[23]WA xlii, 94, 95 (Lectures on Genesis, 1535-45).
[24]WA xxxi, I, 407, 408 (Exposition of Psalm 111, 1530).
[25]WA xl, I, 173, 174 (Commentary on Galatians, 1535).
[26]WA xliii, 548 (Lectures on Genesis, 1535-45).

ters, judges, and hangmen. Yet for this worldly purpose God uses civil authority. . . . God could also build houses of wood and stone without employing any men for this, and He could beget children without fathers and mothers, as He showed when he created Adam and Eve without benefit of parents. But He created man for this purpose and begets and nurses children through parents. . . . God could also make people godly without preachers, but He does not wish to; He wills that the office remain in order that preachers may be His helpers."[27]

In these passages Luther alluded to three major spheres in which God continued to act in history through others. Sometimes he called them God's "orders," and sometimes, looking at them from the horizontal perspective, he called them "estates," stations in life or places which human beings actually occupy.[28] In either case he regarded them as God-given and inescapable facts of human existence. One of these "orders" revolves about man's family relationships, and one may say that at its center are man's biological nature and needs. It includes the sex relations of men and women, the begetting and training of children, the provision of food, clothing, shelter, and similar necessities of life. This was Luther's "economic order," or "order of the household," or *oeconomia*. A second "order" revolves about man's civil relationships, and one may say that at its center are man's social nature and needs. It includes both the exercise of civil authority and the acceptance of such authority, ruling and being ruled, the preservation of external order and the punishment of external crimes. This was Luther's "political order" or *politeia*. A third "order"

---

[27]WA xxxiv, III, 244, 245 (Sermon, 1531).

[28]There is a large literature on this many-sided subject. See especially Franz Lau, *"Aeusserliche Ordnung" und "Weltlich Ding" in Luthers Theologie* (Göttingen, 1933), and Gustaf Wingren, *Luther on Vocation,* tr. by C. C. Rasmussen (Philadelphia, 1957).

revolves about man's relationship to God, and one may say that at its center are man's spiritual nature and needs. It includes the provision and the use of opportunities for teaching and worship, church organization and administration, ministry and laity. This was Luther's "ecclesiastical order" or *ecclesia*.

Luther did not think of these three "orders" or "estates" as sharply separated. They are simply different functions or activities of human life, and any one person is usually involved in all of them, for he may at the same time be a husband and father in the home, a farmer in the economy, a citizen in the state, and a hearer of God's Word as a member of a church. It is also important to observe that in Luther's thinking these "orders" are at once divine creations and human institutions. God commanded men to be fruitful and multiply, and He effects what He commanded through the mutual attraction of the sexes, yet not only is procreation also the work of human beings but the forms which marriage and family life take are shaped by man in history. Civil authority and the sword were ordained by God, yet not only are rule and obedience the works of men but the forms of government and law are determined by changing circumstances in human history. The church as the body of Christ was instituted by God, who calls men into it through the proclamation of the Gospel, yet the ecclesiastical offices, activities, and organizations which have been developed in great variety down through the centuries are as much the inventions of men as are the forms of civil government.

In home and family, therefore, in economic and civil life, in state and church God normally acts through His creatures. But this is not apparent to reason or observation, for God hides His work under His creatures. He acts "under the veil and covering of man and horse. . . . All

creatures are God's masks and masquerades"[29] behind
which He conceals Himself. "The magistrate, emperor,
king, prince, consul, doctor, preacher, teacher, pupil, father, mother, children, master, servant, etc., are *personae*
or masks whom God wishes to be acknowledged and re-
spected as His creatures and as persons who must exist in
this life."[30] In time of common danger God would not have
us sit idly by and await a miracle; He expects us to take
up arms. "He wishes me to do my part," Luther said, "to
have horse, spear, sword, and wagon. . . . He wishes to be
with you and to conceal Himself under these things so that
other people may think that you will prevail by your own
power and preparations for war, although God alone ac-
complishes it."[31] Not only is man an active participant in
history, therefore, but God, too, is present and active; but
God is hidden from human sight and understanding. And
since God hides rather than reveals Himself in historical
events, we should not expect the study of history to lead
to or culminate in God's revelation of Himself. "Every
creature is a disguise and mask of God. So wisdom is
necessary to distinguish God from the mask. . . . In all
such persons God leaves sins and shortcomings, even great
ones, which should warn us to distinguish between the
mask and God Himself. David, the best king, fell into
horrible sins—adultery, murder, etc.—lest he should appear as a person in whom one should put one's trust."[32]

While God is active but hidden in history, man is active
and visible within the structures which God established to
preserve and continue His creation. It is not as if man is
entirely free to act or not according to his pleasure. There
is an element of compulsion in the "orders" and "estates,"

[29]WA xvii, II, 192 (Lenten Postil, 1525).
[30]WA xl, I, 175 (Commentary on Galatians, 1535).
[31]WA xvi, 263 (Sermons on Exodus, 1524-27).
[32]WA xl, I, 174, 175 (Commentary on Galatians, 1535).

31

and to this extent unbelievers as well as believers, evil as well as good men, do God's will. Luther described God as a restless actor who does not allow His creatures to be idle.[33] "God does not wish to rule any longer according to His extraordinary power or, as the sophists say, according to His absolute power, but rather through His creatures, whom He does not wish to be idle. So He provides food, not as He did to the Jews in the wilderness, whom He gave heavenly manna, but through our labor when we do the work of our calling diligently. Nor does He wish any longer to fashion men from lumps of clay, as in the case of Adam, but He employs the union of husband and wife, which He blesses.[34] As Luther once put it, "God does not want things to be done without my work. He does not want me to sit at home, to be idle, to command the dear Lord, and to expect a roasted chicken to fly into my mouth." [35] Man is intended to be God's helper, a cooperator with God. "God does not work without us, for He has renewed us and preserves us for this very purpose, that He may work in us and we may cooperate with Him. Hence through us He preaches, through us He shows mercy to the poor, through us He comforts the sorrowful."[36] As the Large Catechism puts it, our parents, rulers, and others are "the hand, the channel, and the means" by which God gives us all things.[37] This makes man an active participant and gives him a responsible role in history.

Moreover, man is given responsible participation in history for a purpose, and this is the service of his fellowmen. "God does not bestow His gifts on men in order that they

[33]WA xviii, 710 (Bondage of the Will, 1525).
[34]WA xliii, 71 (Lectures on Genesis, 1535-45).
[35]WA xvi, 263 (Sermons on Exodus, 1524-27).
[36]WA xviii, 754 (Bondage of the Will, 1525).
[37]Large Catechism, I, 26.

become insolent and rage against the poor and unfortunate, but whatever He gives, whether it be wealth or power or rule, God gives for His own glory and the benefit of neighbors. Therefore, the purpose of God's gifts is not the pleasure and tyranny of those who receive them. But their legitimate use is directed toward the glory of God and the welfare and benefit of the neighbor. . . . A magistrate is held in honor in order that he may be useful to the commonwealth. A husband and wife are joined together that they may beget and bring up offspring for domestic and public service."[38] In these external, temporal, worldly, bodily things man is not a servant but a lord. Although a sinner, "man has the inclination, reason, free will, and power to build a house, hold public office, run a ship, and perform other functions which are subject to man. These things are not taken away from man."[39] Accordingly there is no necessary difference between the activity of Christians and non-Christians. The Word of God does not teach how a maid or servant are to work, how a burgomaster should rule, or how a farmer should plow or make hay.[40] Nor does the Word of God teach how civil authority is to be exercised or regulated, except that it is to be honored. Hence Christians can learn from the experience of the heathen, who are often more skillful than Christians.[41] Food and drink, observed Luther, "do nothing more because children say grace before and after meals, for godless and rude people who do not say grace (that is, who neither pray to God nor thank Him" get as fat and strong from their eating and drinking as do Christians."[42] Luther went so far as to suggest that in worldly matters rulers should

[38] WA xliii, 505 (Lectures on Genesis, 1535-45).
[39] WA xl, I, 293 (Commentary on Galatians, 1535).
[40] WA xxxii, 304 (Sermons on Matthew, 1530-32).
[41] WA li, 242, 243 (Exposition of Psalm 101, 1534-35).
[42] WA 1, 649 (The Councils and the Churches, 1539).

do all things that pertain to their office, should lock gates, guard towers and walls, secure armaments, and store provisions, and should "act as if there were no God and they had themselves to save and rule, just as a house-father should work as if he could support himself by his work."[43]

Since sin clouds man's reason and will, what man does is of course not always good and right. Lust and infidelity appear in marriage, tyranny and disobedience occur in civil society, usury and deceit arise in economic life, anti-christian prelacy and heresy disturb the church. The offices or functions, said Luther, "are divine and right, but those who are in them and use them are usually of the devil."[44] However, abuses do not abrogate divine institutions. Although corrupted by sin, the process of generation continues.[45] Although kings and kingdoms must fall, authority, reason, and right remain.[46] It often happens that rulers are overthrown but the people and the land remain. "From the beginning of the world until now," observed Luther, "we see that one king is always thrown down by another, one lord by another. . . . God always takes the sword from the fist of one after another on account of their abuse of the sword and gives it to somebody else. Thus the sword and authority always remain in the world, but the persons who rule must again and again be toppled head over heels as they deserve."[47]

In this way God preserves His "orders" from being so abused and corrupted that they cease to be divine institutions. Abuses do not remain unpunished in the long run,

---

[43]WA xv, 372, 373 (Psalm 127 Expounded for the Christians in Riga, 1524).

[44]WA li, 254 (Exposition of Psalm 101, 1534-35).

[45]WA xlii, 54 (Lectures on Genesis, 1535-45).

[46]WA vii, 590 (The Magnificat, 1521).

[47]WA xix, 360 (Prophet Habakkuk Expounded, 1526).

34

although God is patient and long-suffering and we may not be able to discern the connection.[48] God does not leave the world entirely to the clever counsels of men.[49] Things do not always turn out as men plan anyhow. The saying that man proposes but God disposes is therefore true.[50] However, men should not expect God to intervene until they have exhausted their own resources. When their powers are at an end they do well to pray, although their prayer may not prescribe how God should help.[51] Change sometimes occurs in the most unexpected ways, as when the powerful Goliath was overcome by a simple shepherd boy with a sling. In fact, the great turning-points in history often result from the appearance and activity of extraordinary leaders, "miracle-working" individuals of heroic mold who are in God's hands.[52]

Inasmuch as God acts in it, history is the "remembrance of divine work and judgment, how God preserves, governs, hinders, furthers, punishes, and honors the world, and especially men," and we learn this not only from the Scriptures but also from the writings of the pagans.[53] The historian can hardly describe what happened without acknowledging that there is a God who is the creator and preserver of the world, an actor in human history. But he cannot infer from this what God is really like. "Although God is everywhere in all creatures and I might find Him in a stone, in fire, in the water, or in a rope, for He is certainly there, yet He does not wish me to look for Him without the Word. He does not wish me to throw myself into the fire or water or hang myself on the rope. God is every-

---

[48]WA li, 206, 207 (Exposition of Psalm 101, 1534-35); WA xlii, 213, 386 (Lectures on Genesis, 1535-45).

[49]WA li, 203 (Exposition of Psalm 101, 1534-35).

[50]WA xl, III, 209 (Psalms of Degrees, 1532-33).

[51]WA xliv, 648 (Lectures on Genesis, 1535-45).

[52]WA li, 207-214 (Exposition of Psalm 101, 1534-35).

[53]WA 1, 384 (Preface to Capella's History, 1538).

where, but He does not wish you to grope after Him everywhere. You should seek after God where the Word is, and there you will apprehend Him aright. For this reason He provided us with a certain way in which we should seek and find Him, namely, the Word."[54] History, to repeat, is not as such revelation of God, for God remains hidden in it.

Conversation at Luther's table once turned to the possibility of the conversion of the Turks. He declared that he would like to see it but did not expect to. Perhaps, he added, some of those who were then listening to him might live to see it. "If God wills it," he said, "the Turks' barbarity will be no impediment. . . . Who knows what God will do? He is able to accomplish it. His plans are beyond our understanding. He is a wonderful God. We cannot say, for it is written, 'You shall not see my face [Ex. 33:23], you cannot know what I have in mind.' Not until you see it will you know. Who would have thought that the pope would be despised in Germany as he is now? If somebody had suggested this a few years ago, no one would have believed him."[55]

This was a casual testimony of Luther to the unpredictability of history, which is in God's hands even though He chooses to act in history through His creatures. At the same time this is a casual testimony to man's capacity to know and describe what has actually happened, the possibility of investigating and recording history. "Not until you see it will you know." Once something has happened on the plane of the creatures through whom God acts in history, it is visible, though God is not. Humanly discernible occurrences are always concrete, "what happened to

---

[54]WA xix, 492 (Sermon on the Sacrament, 1526).
[55]WA TR v, 5536 (1542-43).

this city, this kingdom, this prince, this man, this woman."[56]
Only such things on the horizontal plane provide the stuff
with which the historian can deal. He works not with principles and generalizations but with events, whether they
be deeds or thoughts—not with the genus or the species, as
Luther put it, but with what is singular and non-recur-
ring.[57] For this reason whatever has been said or done must
always be observed in its historical context.[58] A good historian must be an individual with a lion's heart who dares
to record the truth which he finds. He must not omit to
record evil in order to please his lords and friends, nor
must he exaggerate the good they do. He must not paint
his native land in colors which are too favorable, nor
describe the enemies of his native land in terms which
reflect bias. Distorted accounts of history make it hard for
people to know what to believe. One must therefore treat
unreliable historians as one treats those who adulterate
wine with water.[59]

This is the substance of what we may learn about the
study of history from Luther. Belief in God does not
militate against historical investigation by rendering it
impossible or unnecessary; rather, it encourages us to seek
wisdom for our earthly life in the record of mankind's
experiences.[60] Theoretically at least, a Christian's description of the past will not differ from that of a non-Christian
who employs the same rigid methodology. Difference will
emerge only in the judgments which are expressed, for the
Christian historian's judgments should be informed by the
Word of God. On the other hand, it is not possible to come
to faith in God by way of historical research and study, for

[56]WA xv, 45 (To the Councilmen of all Cities, 1524).
[57]WA 1, 5 (Preface to Barnes's Lives of the Popes, 1536).
[58]WA xxx, II, 108-110 (War against the Turk, 1529).
[59]WA 1, 385 (Preface to Capella's History, 1538).
[60]WA xv, 45 (To the Councilmen of all Cities, 1524).

ultimately not only God Himself but even believers and the church remain hidden to the eyes of the historian in his role as historian.[61] We cannot use God (or "the hand of God") as a principle or criterion for the interpretation of historical events without denying the hiddenness of His activity in history.

---

[61]WA xviii, 652 (Bondage of the Will, 1525).

The Professor of Theology

T HE reform of the church in the sixteenth century was accompanied by a reform of education. One might say that this was inevitable, if for no other reason than that a different understanding of the Christian faith required a different kind of training for life. We can see this most clearly in the sharp contrast between the demands made on the evangelical ministry and those made on the medieval priesthood. "Our office," wrote Luther in the preface to his Small Catechism, "has now assumed a very different character from that which it bore under the pope."[1]

It was also natural, if not inevitable, that the reform of higher education should first assume concrete form in the University of Wittenberg, where, as Luther once put it, "God revealed His Word."[2] The outward structure of the

---

[1] Small Catechism, Preface, 26.
[2] WA TR iv, 5126 (1540).

medieval university was preserved.[3] There was an arts faculty, usually called a faculty of philosophy, which was preparatory for the three professional faculties or colleges of theology, law, and medicine. The college of theology was the largest of the three "higher faculties" in point of the number of students and instructors, although the college of arts was of course even larger because students were required to pass through it before they could begin their study of theology, law, or medicine.

Within this inherited structure reforms were introduced in the several curricula of the university under the impetus of the Reformation; these changes were initiated by Luther and then progressively developed especially by his colleague Philip Melanchthon. Put in simple terms, the reforms consisted of the substitution of philology for philosophy as the core of instruction. The study of Greek and Hebrew was introduced alongside of Latin, and to a large extent original texts were read in these languages instead of medieval translations of them and medieval commentaries on them. Here the influence of Renaissance humanism asserted itself. In the college of theology scholastic philosophy and theology were supplanted by biblical exegesis and exposition, and the earlier preoccupation with a second-hand knowledge of Aristotle was reduced. The academic statutes prepared in 1533 sum up the reforms which had gradually been introduced during the preceding fifteen years by asserting that Latin, Greek, and Hebrew were taught "in order to show, in so far as possible, what is written in the sources and what the true and genuine meaning of words in the sources is. God gave the

---

[3]For general treatments of the University of Wittenberg see Walter Friedensburg, *Geschichte der Universität Wittenberg* (Halle, 1917), and Kurt Aland, "Die theologische Fakultät Wittenberg," in *Festschrift zur 450-Jahrfeier der Martin Luther Universität Halle-Wittenberg* (Halle, 1953).

gift of languages to the church for the ministry of the Gospel, and often restored it. He does not wish that what He restored should be lost through neglect, but rather that by reasonable diligence and study it be preserved for the sake of the common need of the church."[4] The importance of the sources for an understanding of philosophy and history was also emphasized, and students in the college of theology were to study not only "prophetic and apostolic books, but also the history of controversies in the church."[5]

Although always keenly interested in what was going on in other faculties of the university—he had many observations to offer about the arts, law, and medicine—Luther was a professor of theology. For the last ten years of his life he was also dean of the theological faculty. Teaching was, strictly speaking, his calling. However, he did not think of his teaching as restricted to the lecture hall in the university. He thought of himself as a teacher of the church, and he instructed countless people through the medium of his publications, through his tireless preaching, and through his private counsel. We shall have occasion to see that Luther's contact with his students in the university also took all these forms; they met him in the classroom, read his books, listened to his sermons, visited his home, and in a variety of ways benefited from his counsel.

Largely as a result of the stir Luther was making, the enrollment of students in Wittenberg reached its height in 1520, when Luther wrote to his friend George Spalatin, "The number of students increases daily, the little town cannot hold them all, and many are forced to leave again."[6] At this time about 400 students were attending Luther's

---

[4] CR x, 1007.
[5] CR x, 994, 1002.
[6] WA Br i, 96 (May 1, 1520).

41

lectures. The flourishing condition did not last. In the decade of the twenties a decline in enrollments set in. This was due to a number of factors which affected all the German universities: discouragement of begging, which had formerly helped support students; reaction against humanism's artificial enthusiasm for formal education; insistence on the part of some religious radicals that manual labor is preferable to study; and effects of the Peasants' War and recurring pestilence. Enrollments at Wittenberg continued to outstrip those at other German universities, whether Protestant or Catholic, but it was not until Luther's later years that they returned to about the level of the year 1520.

There was no such thing in those days as an entrance examination. However, students who went to Wittenberg for their arts studies were expected to be able to read, write, understand, and speak Latin, the academic language of the time,[7] and they developed proficiency in the use of this tongue while there. The employment of a common language made it possible for students to come from all parts of Europe. John Mathesius, who went to Wittenberg in 1529, reported that among his fellow students, in addition to those from various German lands, there were young men from Denmark, Sweden, Lithuania, Holland, Poland, Bohemia, Hungary, Transylvania, Russia, Greece, Italy, France, Spain, England, and Scotland.[8] Students from such varied nationalities and dissimilar backgrounds were naturally different in their tastes, dress, and customs, and it was reported by the university authorities that it was "difficult to make them conform."[9] Even the universal

---

[7] CR x, 1016, 1019.

[8] Martin Huerlimann, ed., *Martin Luther, dargestellt von seinen Freunden und Zeitgenossen* (Berlin, 1933), p. 187.

[9] Walter Friedensburg, ed., *Urkundenbuch der Universität Wittenberg* (Magdeburg, 1926), Vol. I, p. 239.

use of Latin did not always assure understanding on account of varying regional pronunciations of this language.[10] Special provision had to be made for foreigners who could not follow German services, and the occasional introduction of German into lectures must have dismayed some auditors, however much it helped others.[11]

It was not until the seventeenth century that theology was divided into the four disciplines of biblical, historical, systematic, and practical theology. During most of Luther's career in Wittenberg four men taught in the theological faculty, assisted now and then on a part-time basis by members of the philosophical faculty. But after the reform of theological study in Luther's time, all four professors lectured on the Bible, two on Old Testament books and two on New Testament books alternately. Some provision was nevertheless made for occasional lectures on Augustine's *The Spirit and the Letter* "in order to set forth the right understanding of grace in Paul,"[12] or on the Nicene Creed "so that the students may see that the teaching of our churches is in agreement with that of purer antiquity and the true church of God."[13] As a matter of fact, as students' notes on Luther's lectures reveal, Luther did not adhere strictly to what we should today call biblical exegesis and exposition. He introduced historical, systematic, and practical materials, and therefore the concentration on biblical studies did not represent quite such a narrow reduction as the university statutes might at first sight suggest.

Professors of theology were obliged by the statutes "to lecture an hour a day, four days a week, namely, on Mon-

---

[10]Cf. William B. Rye, ed., *England as Seen by Foreigners in the Days of Elizabeth* (London, 1865), pp. xxxvi, xxxvii.

[11]Ratzeberger, *op. cit.*, pp. 80, 81. Cf. WA TR iv, 3947, 4020.

[12]Friedensburg, *Urkundenbuch, I*, 174, 175.

[13]CR x, 1003.

day, Tuesday, Thursday, and Friday."[14] Luther did not adhere strictly to this requirement, for sometimes he lectured more often and sometimes less often.[15] Besides, his lectures were omitted entirely from time to time when he was absent on account of illness or for other reasons. Toward the end of his life, when he was often sick and away on journeys, he once covered only three chapters of Genesis in two years.[16] If this appears to be a light teaching load it must be remembered that Luther was breaking new ground and that only in the case of Galatians and the Psalms did he lecture on the same book of the Bible more than once. Moreover, lecturing represented only part of his teaching load.

What must appear somewhat strange to us today is that no attempt was made by the lecturers to cover a major part of the Bible in every student generation. Moreover, the treatment of a book of the Bible was seldom begun and ended within the limits of an academic year or of the quarters into which the academic year was divided. The pace was leisurely, and a course of lectures simply continued until the lecturer was ready to come to an end. Moreover, courses were sometimes changed or interrupted at the whim of the instructor. For example, while lecturing on Genesis, Luther reached the narrative about Joseph in Chapter 37 by the middle of December, 1543. He began his next lecture by saying, "Now that the nativity of our Lord is approaching, which should be celebrated with joy in the church, . . . if my health permits I shall suspend my lectures on Joseph and we shall speak during these days of the incarnation of the Son of God."[17] These inserted lectures, based on Isaiah 9, continued for about a

---

[14]Friedensburg, *Urkundenbuch*, I, 174.
[15]Cf., e.g., WA xxvi, 3; WA xl, III, 476.
[16]Mathesius, *op. cit.*, p. 155.
[17]WA xl, III, 597, 598 (Exposition of Isaiah 9, 1543-44).

month, and then Luther returned to his exposition of Genesis where he had left off. A couple of months later, when Easter was approaching, Luther again interrupted his lectures on Genesis in order to treat Isaiah 53. He began these special lectures by saying, "I have decided to treat Isaiah 53 at this time because it has been specially appointed [as the Epistle for Good Friday] and so that we may meditate on the passion and resurrection of Christ and may give thanks for His unspeakable gift."[18]

While Luther spoke with great earnestness and assurance about such convictions of his faith as revolved about man's sin and God's grace, he allowed considerable latitude for divergent opinions on the part of his students and others. "This," he said with reference to a passage in Zechariah, "is obscure. It has been expounded by others in many different ways, and as a result it has become even more obscure. I allow everyone to have his honor and thank him for his efforts. I shall also present what I understand the meaning to be until somebody else does it better."[19] While lecturing on Genesis he often had occasion to say, "I freely confess that I do not know," or "For myself I would not attempt to settle anything on this point."[20] With reference to Nicholas Lyra's opinion on the meaning of a term he said, "Whether this is true or false means nothing to me. I prefer not to believe it, but I shall let him have his opinion."[21] Luther was also frank to confess changes in his own judgments, as he did when he expressed dissatisfaction with his earlier attempts to expound the Psalms.[22]

When in his later years Luther entered the lecture hall

---

[18]WA xl, III, 686 (Exposition of Isaiah 53, 1544).
[19]WA xxiii, 579 (Prophet Zechariah Expounded, 1527).
[20]WA xlii, 23, 24, 29 et passim (Lectures on Genesis, 1535-45).
[21]WA xl, III, 13 (Psalms of Degrees, 1532-33).
[22]E.g., WA TR ii, 40 (1532).

his students rose from their seats. The observance of this traditional academic practice was suggested by Philip Melanchthon as a gesture of respect. Luther did not like it, and he was reported to have said: "I wish that Master Philip had not bothered to do this. On account of this rising of the students I have to pray more often, and if I dared I would sometimes leave without lecturing. He who seeks honor will not attain it, or if he does, it brings great danger with it."[23] Luther carried with him to the lecture hall the text of the biblical book on which he was to lecture and some outlines and notes written on scraps of paper which he happened to have had at hand when he made his preparations. Some of these notes have fortunately been preserved, and they give us an insight into Luther's method, especially when compared with the notes which students took of the lectures as they were actually delivered. Luther's own notes reveal his diligent use of the Hebrew and Greek texts, for he wrote the meaning of key terms either in the margins of his copy of the Bible or on the slips of paper he took along to his class. In his preparation he also consulted lexical aids, the observations of earlier commentators like Nicholas Lyra, and whatever new sources of knowledge were available to him.[24] An auditor's notes on the lectures on Ecclesiastes indicate that Luther once interrupted his lectures for several days because he encountered difficulties in interpretation. When he resumed the lectures he confessed candidly, "I postponed my lectures on account of the difficulty I ran into. I find no help in commentaries, etc. It cost me great labor to unravel this passage. I lack facility in the language

---

[23]Mathesius, *op. cit.*, pp. 176, 177.

[24]E.g., WA xlviii, 302-323 (Lectures on Titus, 1527). Cf. A. Freitag's introduction to Luther's lectures on the Psalms of Degrees (WA xl, III, 1, 2) and also Peter Meinhold, *Die Genesisvorlesung Luthers und ihre Herausgeber* (Stuttgart, 1936), pp. 180-202.

employed here, for it has its own peculiar forms and figures of speech which cannot be understood apart from experience with the language, since much depends on the syntax."[25] Luther's own notes were usually in the form of pegs for his memory and as points of departure for extemporaneous exposition, elaboration, and application. So his preparatory notes were scant when compared with the much fuller notes which students made of the actual lectures.[26]

As was then customary, the lectures were delivered in Latin. However, in order to make his meaning clear Luther often resorted to German phrases and sentences. He also introduced many off-the-cuff illustrations from his experience, observation, and reading, and he used a variety of anecdotes and analogies. Mount Hermon, he once explained, is a large forest, like the Thuringian Forest.[27] He put himself into his lectures. On one occasion he averred that if he had been in Noah's place before the Flood he would have thrown up his hands in despair, and another time he declared that if he had been in Isaac's shoes, he would not have submitted to being deprived of the promised Rachel.[28] He spoke rapidly and fluently. His own description in his preface to the lectures on Genesis fits what we learn from other sources: "These lectures were delivered in an extemporaneous and popular form, spoken rapidly just as the expressions came to my lips, mixed with German, and surely more verbose than I should wish."[29] A student named John William Reifenstein, who had some

---

[25]WA xx, 121 (Lectures on Ecclesiastes, 1532).

[26]Cf. WA xlviii, 305-312 (Preparatory Notes for Lectures on Titus, 1527), and A. Freitag's introduction to Luther's lectures on I Timothy, WA xxvi, 3 (1528).

[27]WA xl, III, 15 (Psalms of Degrees, 1532-33). Cf. WA xvi, 333 (Sermon, 1525).

[28]WA xlii, 324; WA xliii, 633 (Lectures on Genesis, 1535-45).

[29]WA xlii, 1 (Luther's Preface to the Lectures on Genesis, 1544).

47

artistic gifts, drew a sketch of the lecturing Luther which has come down to us. It pictures Luther standing behind a lecture desk with his left hand resting lightly on the desk and his right hand gesturing freely. The face is earnest but kindly.[30] For the most part Luther's auditors seem to have found his lectures profitable. "I often returned from these lectures," Mathesius confessed, "full of comfort and joy."[31] And Melanchthon testified to Luther's personal involvement when he reported that "his words seemed not merely to pass through his lips but to flow from his heart."[32]

In addition to attending lectures (normally a maximum of three hours a day), students were originally required to engage in weekly disputations, which were often held on Fridays.[33] These, too, were inherited from the Middle Ages. Because the disputations of the medieval scholastics were regarded as having been such an unprofitable beating of the wind, disputations fell into disfavor and disuse when the early reforms were made in the curricula of the several colleges in the University of Wittenberg. However, some were reintroduced in 1533 on the ground that they provided students with opportunities for participation, practice, and reflection. In some respects they may be said to have served a function similar to that of modern seminars. "The exercise of disputations," the university statutes stated, "offers many advantages, for they accustom the student to sum up complicated matters in brief propositions and embrace them appropriately in syllogisms, quiet-

---

[30]WA DB iv, 589, 590. The drawing is reproduced on p. lix.

[31]Mathesius, *op. cit.*, p. 83.

[32]CR x, 161 (Melanchthon's Preface to the Wittenberg edition of Luther's works, 1546).

[33]There is a general discussion of academic disputations in the introduction to Paul Drews, *Disputationen Dr. Martin Luthers in den Jahren 1535-1545* (Göttingen, 1895). Texts of disputations which Luther prepared and participated in are reproduced here and also in WA xxxix, I and II.

ly to search out and clarify obscure things, and to provide skill in discussion and readiness in speech. Consequently we do not wish disputations to be omitted."[34]

Members of the faculty and selected students participated in turn. In the presence of the whole college community the pros and cons of an issue were explored and debated. Theses for disputation were prepared by an instructor, and he also presided at the exercise and introduced the subject in a brief address. An address of this kind delivered by Luther in 1537 throws some light on the atmosphere and conduct of a disputation: "We shall dispute without the least trace of pride or arrogance, attacking and finding fault with nobody, overwhelming nobody with jibes, as some do if another cannot fashion arguments as quickly as they can or expound what he wishes as clearly as they can or refute arguments as sharply as they can. For we are not unaware of the old proverb, 'One learns by making mistakes.' On this account you spectators and auditors ought to be fair to us and not seize an occasion to trick, interrupt, or disturb if anything that is said in the course of the argumentation or is posited or explained by a respondent is not sufficiently clear or appropriate. It often happens that those who watch others in these exercises want to be seen or want to appear to be better, but when they are engaged with us in the same exercise and debate, they see that they, too, are wanting in persuasive proofs. Wherefore I wish in conclusion to remind you who are about to dispute that you rise confidently, spiritedly, and cheerfully and speak your piece freely before us, your teachers, for the sake of God and for the profit of the church, the state, and yourselves. I wish the rest of the auditors to listen to the speakers, quietly and in silence in order that they may be in a position to form

---

[34]CR x, 994.

a fair opinion of us."[35] The university statutes stipulated that foolish and unprofitable topics be avoided; the intention was not disputation for its own sake but search after and instruction in truth.[36] The theses which Luther prepared make it clear that he used the disputations as instruments of instruction in important contemporary issues.

Melanchthon had the reputation of being very severe in his treatment of students in the disputations. Sometimes he became so impatient that he would not hear a floundering student out but would tell him to keep quiet and give another student a chance to speak. At other times, it was reported, he would scold a timid or ill-prepared student and call him "a fool, an ass, a yellow-bill, a stupid dolt who had no sense." Of course, the effect of this was to make such students feel humiliated and discouraged. In contrast, a student described Luther as conducting himself with much more calm and composure. "If somebody advanced a weak, poor, or inept argument, Dr. Luther did not at once reject it, as Philip did, but he took over the argument and often gave it a better turn and shape than had been thought of by the opponent and then asked if this had not been the opponent's real meaning. When the opponent said 'Yes,' Dr. Luther put the argument into syllogistic form so that everybody marveled at it and had much to learn from it." Luther often discussed a problem with a student again and again and did not press the student to agree with him at once.[37] "Disputations," said Luther, "are of great benefit to fellows who study. . . . Accordingly I praise the young students even if their arguments are not in order."[38] Again he said, "Nobody becomes a

<hr />

[35] WA xxxix, I, 271, 272 (Circular Disputation, 1537); Drews, op. cit., p. 170.
[36] CR x, 994.
[37] Ratzeberger, op. cit., pp. 93, 100, 101.
[38] WA TR iv, 4056 (1538).

doctor all at once. There is no tree that was not at first a little shrub. It takes time."[39]

Examinations were as a rule given annually, but only for candidates for a bachelor's or master's degree in the arts college. Candidates for a doctor's degree were examined privately by the dean of the theological faculty and then had to demonstrate their learning in a public doctoral disputation. Although there were few formal examinations, it was apparently as difficult then as it is now to persuade students that examinations were, among other things, a useful incentive to study.[40]

From 1523 to 1533 no degree of doctor of theology was granted in Wittenberg. This was not only "because everything was in confusion on account of the controversy with the pope," as Luther wrote into the records of the university.[41] When the theological curriculum was reformed by discarding medieval scholasticism, there was a tendency to frown on degrees in theology as part and parcel of the rejected system. Moreover, the granting of degrees was sharply attacked by Andrew Carlstadt, a religious radical who was still a member of the Wittenberg faculty when the educational reforms were in progress. After participating in the award of doctor's degrees to two candidates in 1523 Carlstadt had announced publicly that he knew this was a sin, that he had done it simply for the sake of the fees, and that he would never again be party to such an act. Carlstadt contended that the words of Jesus in Matt. 23:8, "Be not ye called rabbi, for one is your master, even Christ, and all ye are brethren," forbade the conferring of academic titles. Luther took exception to what he called these "sacrilegious words" from Carlstadt's

---

[39] WA TR iv, 4193 (1538).
[40] Cf. CR x, 84, 85, 1015.
[41] K. E. Foerstemann, ed., *Liber decanorum facultatis theologiae Academiae Vitebergensis* (Leipzig, 1838), p. 28.

"blasphemous lips."[42] The words of Jesus, (Luther maintained, were not to be understood as meaning that academic titles like "master" and "doctor" were not to be used. Rather, what Jesus meant was in effect this: "You should not invent or produce new teaching but should adhere to what I have taught, and I have commanded you to teach it to others and show it to them."[43]

Luther often asserted the importance of cultivating knowledge and transmitting it to the next generation, and especially of conveying to others a knowledge of the Gospel. This cannot be done well without schools and all that goes with them, including sound teaching, diligent study, and academic advancement. "God wishes that there be schools," Luther wrote once in connection with an academic function, "and from these He selects, chooses, and raises up those who should disseminate His teaching. Therefore the prophets, Christ, and the apostles also had schools. From them we learn what schools are, and we should honor them, furnish them with good practices, and know that this saying of Christ also pertains to the doctors in the schools, 'Where two or three are gathered in my name, there am I in the midst of them' [Matt. 18:20]. Christ is present among our students and guides and helps them in their studies. These things should be considered in public [academic] convocations, and our hearts should be moved to call on Christ that He may be present and aid and direct us."[44]

One of the "good practices" which Luther may well have had in mind here was the granting of academic degrees in course. He joined Melanchthon in urging that the award of degrees be restored and that the act be clothed

---

[42]*Ibid.*, p. 27.
[43]WA TR v, 6207; cf. WA xlii, 417 (Lectures on Genesis, 1535-45).
[44]WA Br x, 585 (1545).

52

with the dignity it deserved.[45] From 1533 to Luther's death in 1546 degrees in theology were conferred almost every year. The requirement for the degree was attendance at lectures in the college of theology for six years, followed by a private examination by the dean and a public doctoral disputation.[46] A typical announcement, posted on the university bulletin board by Luther as dean of the theological faculty in 1545, reads in part like this: "On the coming seventeenth day of September the testimony of our college will be publicly announced with reference to the studies and the [doctor's] degree of that honorable man Master Peter Hegemann. We therefore request all honorable persons who esteem the ministry of the Gospel to assemble in the customary place for this award of the degree. . . ."[47]

The "customary place" was the Castle Church, where degrees were conferred by the dean whenever candidates were ready. A formula like the following, prepared by Luther, was used: "By virtue of apostolic and divine authority and also by virtue of the authority of empire and state (both of which are divine, the one heavenly and the other earthly), I call, pronounce, and declare you to be a doctor of sacred theology in the name of the Father and of the Son and of the Holy Spirit. This is said in order that you may be mindful of the Lord who has called you and of what and how great He is, and also that you may be mindful of those against whom you have been called, of what sort and how powerful they are, so that you may be a leader, messenger, and ambassador of God against the adversaries of Him who sends you, even as I have been sent. The Lord strengthen you, and may you be strong.

---

[45]WA TR ii, 2788b (1532).
[46]WA Br xi, 175 (1545).
[47]CR x, 1004, 1005.

Be not afraid. The Lord be with you. Amen."[48] Not only the place in which the exercises were held but also the form of these words will suggest the extent to which the academic atmosphere was colored by the ecclesiastical. The university statutes emphasized the relation of the theological faculty to the evangelical ministry and the obligation of all professors and doctors of theology to the doctrinal consensus of the church.[49] The distinction between the award of a degree of doctor of theology and ordination (which was first observed in Wittenberg in 1531) was somewhat tenuous. Of course, by no means all candidates for ordination were candidates for the doctor's degree. Whenever a call was available and a student appeared to be ready to fill it, he was recommended for ordination after a private examination by the dean. Ecclesiastical as well as academic procedures were comparatively free and flexible at that time.

When after the lapse of a decade the conferring of degrees was resumed in 1533, Elector John Frederick of Saxony attended the "solemn ceremony" and "gave a splendid feast . . . to all the doctors and masters and many students of theology," the guests filling eighteen or twenty tables. Such banquets traditionally followed the ceremony, "as ancient custom had handed it down."[50] When, two years later, degrees were conferred on Jerome Weller and Nicholas Medler, the elector at Luther's request sent venison and five buckets and seven quarts of the best wine, Justus Jonas sent an assortment of poultry, and Luther's wife Katie prepared the banquet, at which guests filled seven or eight tables.[51]

---

[48]WA xlviii, 701 (No. 7168). This form was prepared by Luther in 1533.

[49]CR x, 1002, 1003, 1011.

[50]Foerstemann, *op. cit.*, pp. 29, 30.

[51]WA Br vii, 223, 232 (1535); Foerstemann, *op. cit.*, p. 31; Georg Buchwald, "Lutherana: Notizen aus Rechnungsbüchern des Thürin-

Luther enjoyed such convivial occasions. As he did elsewhere when he was in an expansive mood, he mingled wit with wisdom and undoubtedly gave the students who were present, as well as the "new doctors," hints on study and learning and their careers. "To say much with few words is an art," he once suggested with an eye on future preachers, "but it is great folly to use many words and still say nothing."[52] "Learning which is neglected and not put to use is nothing," he said another time, "for there is little difference between a pretty girl who has no suitor and an ugly girl."[53] On still another occasion he recommended that it is better to study a few books thoroughly than read many books cursorily. "A student who does not wish to squander his efforts ought so to read and re-read some good author that the author enters into his flesh and blood. Reading many books will confuse rather than instruct. . . . A person who lives everywhere lives nowhere."[54] Again, he suggested that to study without putting one's heart into it is as much wasted effort as to drink without thirst or to pray without devotion.[55] Luther could not divest himself of his mantle as teacher even when his students were celebrating the end of their formal studies and their departure from the university.

gischen Staatsarchivs zu Weimar," *Archiv für Reformationsgeschichte,* XXV (1928), p. 87.

[52]WA TR iv, 4426 (1539).
[53]WA TR iii, 3021 (1533).
[54]WA TR iii, 2894a (1533).
[55]WA TR v, 5607 (undated).

Willem J. Kooiman

Luther's
Later Years

Luther at Home

Luther as He Saw Himself

Luther at the End of His Days

Luther at Home

MARTIN LUTHER was a man of utmost constancy. How sound of character he was we can see from the fact that he was the same man under all circumstances: in his study the same as on the platform, at the table the same as in the pulpit, among the members of his family the same as among princes and prelates.

Luther practiced what he preached and he meant what he wrote. From his appearance in public and from his writings we can already get to know the man completely; they bear the stamp of his individuality, his personality. But just because his private life and his life in public form such a close unity, it is extremely useful for the knowledge not only of his character but also of his theology and philosophy of life, to consider him in his normal everyday life at home. Then it will be clear that his domestic life was an integral part of his confession and public testimony.

There are few historical personages whose home life is better known to us than that of the reformer. In his years of maturity we can follow him practically from day to day in all his doings,[1] thanks to his extensive correspondence, in which even rather intimate details are given, and to the diaries of his table-companions, who noted down even the cries he uttered when his kidneys troubled him.

A remarkable family it was, living in the unfinished building of the former Augustinian monastery. It had something artistic. A hospitable home, with many guests and little money. We might call it Bohemian, if we were not constantly reminded of the Middle Ages by a strictness of form and morals. At any rate, the fashion of the Protestant rectory with its bourgeois correctness and quiet austerity did not originate in Luther's home; that is rather something dating from the pietistic days with Spener, its originator.

When we enter the Black Cloister we find family life flourishing. Luther and his wife—his junior by fifteen years—have come to understand each other completely, after a decennium of marriage with all its joys and sorrows. Two strong personalities who both of them know what they want, but who know above all that they belong together. There is nothing strained or sentimental in this marriage, it is normal, strong, honest and sober.

The Dutch Professor J. Huizinga, in his book *The Waning of the Middle Ages*, has clearly shown how sexual love and eroticism were real elements of the cultural pattern of the late Middle Ages, but at the same time how mutual faithfulness and readiness to make sacrifices did not count for much with the partners. In this respect, because of the conspicuous place he occupied, Luther's doctrines and the example he set have become of great importance. He showed by words and

[1] Georg Buchwald, *Luther-Kalendarium*. Leipzig, 1929[2].

deeds that the essence of love between the two partners should be faithfulness and readiness to sacrifice, both physically and spiritually.

The sexual relations between husband and wife are part and parcel of this kind of love. It is certainly completely wrong to make a distinction in this respect between the "younger" and the "older" Luther. It has been said that when he was young the sexual side of marriage was all important to him, and that marriage was a means of preventing lechery more than anything else, but that after his storm-and-stress period a kind of sublimated sexuality, a more spiritual contemplation of marriage took the place of his former, more sensually directed, views.

This is an incorrect conception, because the distinction between spirit and flesh incorporated in it does not hold good for Luther. The question whether the relations between husband and wife are physical or spiritual did not occur to him. The distinction physical as opposed to mental or spiritual was something he was not aware of. The Luther research which tries to analyze his marriage ethics with the help of these notions is working with a formula of an idealistic-humanistic philosophy of life quite alien to our reformer.

All Luther wants to show, in his life and in his doctrines, is the way in which husband and wife, in the sexual as well as in other aspects of their married life, can fulfill the task assigned to them by God, a task that in the first place consists in the begetting and bringing up of children.[2] In doing so he continually sees man as a physical-spiritual totality, and as such places him, also in the husband-wife relation, before the face of the

[2]WA, xlii, 89 (Lecture on Genesis, 1535-1545).

Lord, *coram Deo*. For his religious faith everything on this earth, including sexual life if not misused, is pure and sacred. It is especially in this being-together of husband and wife that God Himself does His work. Sexual life does not need to be hallowed by asceticism, nor marriage by making a sacrament of it. They are placed on the solid ground of God's creation, and are sanctified only by the grace of God.[3]

It has to be admitted, though, that with respect to his sexual life Luther had greater difficulty, in the paradox of the flesh, to discover the hidden meaning of God than he had with respect to his family life. But after all he saw, in married life more than anywhere else, God working in His creation. When trying to demonstrate the all-sufficiency, the all-inclusive activity of God, this important aspect of his theological ideas, he prefers to take his illustrations from married life, the family. There one can see so very clearly that man can do nothing, God everything. God uses husband and wife, marriage and the family, in order to be the absolute and sovereign God who creates all from nothing and perpetually realizes His plans of creation in the meeting of the sexes and in the relation between parents and children.

It is well known what an important part the theory of the realms plays in Luther's theology. In general he distinguishes two realms, the spiritual and the temporal. In the spiritual kingdom God works directly by means of the preaching of His Word. In the temporal realm

[3]Olavi Lähteenmäki, *Sexus und Ehe bei Luther* (Schriften der Luther-Agricola-Gesellschaft, 10), Turku, 1955. It is curious that Albert Hyma, *New Light on Martin Luther*, Grand Rapids, 1958, 237, says that Luther's view on married life and the monastic vow of chastity have seldom been discussed by Protestant biographers. Lähteenmäki gives much literature.

He uses regulations of society and intermediaries, employed and appointed by Him.

According to Luther, marriage and the family definitely belong to the temporal realm. The liberation of married life and family life from the fetters of sacraments and the jurisdiction of the church was, as we know, one of the most important results of his reformation. What matters in marriage is "something external, physical and temporal," a regulation imposed by God in His creation. This is preeminently the domain where man may and must adapt himself to the service of God independently, without supervision by the church.

But at times Luther also makes use of the triple division, the three realms, the estates of church, family and government, *tria visibilia regiment, Grundordnungen, Hierarchien, ecclesia, oeconomia, politia.*[4] The *Hausstand* or home life then takes a middle position between the realms temporal and spiritual; it is the connecting link between those two. From this one can see the important place married life and family life occupy with him. The realms temporal and spiritual converge in the home life. Luther said with great emphasis that the family is the basis and the origin of the state. The state is a family, the monarch is a father, both on a large scale. When discussing the fourth Commandment in the Large Catechism he says that parental authority is the origin of all authority of worldly governments.[5] He speaks of the founding and development of the community, the school and the government in this manner: There was a father who could not control one of his sons. He sought help

[4] WA, ii, 734 (Ein Sermon von dem Sakrament der Taufe, 1519); WA, xxvi, 504 (Vom Abendmahl Christi, Bekenntnis, 1528); WA, xx (2), 155 (Large Catechism, 1529); WA, 1, 652 (Von den Konziliis und Kirchen, 1539); WA, xxxix (2), 34 (Disputatio 9-5-1539).

[5] WA, xxx (1), 152 (Large Catechism, 4th Commandment).

from a neighbor. Realizing no success, the father solicited the help of a schoolmaster. Since the son continued in his disobedient ways, the father employed the services of a man who, for the first time, became a policeman. So, in concentric circles paternal authority extends to that of the government.[6] But at the same time Luther is able to state that the family forms the basis and germ-seed of the church. In the introduction to his *Hauspostille*, a collection of sermons preached in the family circle, he says that the divine service in the home was the origin of the church service. The patriarchs preached in their tents to children and servants. The neighbors dropped in to listen. Thus originated the religious community.[7] To Luther, the family Bible is not a small-scale pulpit Bible; rather the Bible of the pulpit is a large-scale family Bible.

Marriage and the family are matters of the world, yet they can be called a spiritual estate.[8] More than any others they form the most noble and general *Christenstand*, "Christian estate." The temporal and spiritual estates, whether they concern emperors, kings or bishops, have to submit to this ordination of God.[9] The position of the parents is superior even to that of kings inasmuch as temporal and spiritual power are combined in them. The parents have temporal power, being parents, and they have also spiritual power, being apostles and bishops in their home.[10] This applies especially to the father, who

---

[6]Edmund Schlink, *Theologie der lutherischen Bekenntnisschriften*, München, 1940, 322 ff.; Johannes Heckel, *Lex Charitatis. Eine juristische Untersuchung über das Recht in der Theologie Martin Luthers*, München, 1953, 108.

[7]Georg Buchwald, *Mratin Luther als Kind, Vater und Freund*. Berlin, 1957, 121.

[8]Gustaf Wingren, *Luthers Lehre vom Beruf*. München, 1952, 84.

[9]WA, xxx (1), 162 (Large Catechism, 6th Commandment).

[10]WA, x (2), 301 (Vom ehelichen Leben, 1522).

takes the place of God in his family. The father is "God, Lord, judge and teacher of his children."[11]

It is against this background that we shall have to consider Luther as the father of a family. The authority with which he acts has a deeper ground than "the patriarchism which he inherited from the ancient world" and the obedience he exacts is of a character different from that exacted by an "oriental monarch."[12] They are closely bound up with his theories of the realms, which in their turn are linked up with his ideas about the all-sufficiency, the all-inclusive activity of God.

Luther once wrote to a friend, a henpecked husband, who complained that he was completely under the domination of his wife, "That is your own fault, you have given in too much to her and spoiled her. You should have remembered that a man should obey God more than he should his wife, which means that you should not have allowed the prestige of the man, being the image and glory of God (I Corinthians 11:7), to be trampled under foot by her."[13]

Katharina von Bora was a strong-willed woman, self-confident and energetic. She came of a family of the landed gentry and during her time in the nunnery of Nimbschen she had been very active. With a firm hand she conducted the enormous household in Wittenberg with its numerous inmates and guests. With alertness, thrift and intelligence, she ran not only the kitchen but also the brewery and the stables of the Black Monastery, where, in the year 1542, Luther kept 5 cows, 9 calves, 4 goats, 13 pigs and several horses. Quite a farming industry! Besides all that there were a fish pond, various

---

[11]WA, xvi, 490 (Predigten über das zweite Buch Mose, 1524-27).

[12]Albert Hyma, *op. cit.*, 237.

[13]Julius Köstlin, *Martin Luther, sein Leben und seine Schriften*. Berlin, 1903, II, 488.

gardens in the city and fields outside the gates of the town, plus the farm Zulsdorf near Borna, Kate's favorite property. She must indeed have been a very energetic woman to be able to run such an extensive concern.

And Luther was only too glad to leave all this to her. He teased her sometimes about her preference for her gardens and farm, especially by means of self-invented nicknames which he gave her in his letters: "To the rich lady of Zulsdorf, my beloved wife, Katharina, Mrs. Dr. Luther, mistress of the pigmarket, who lives in the flesh at Wittenberg, but in the spirit at Zulsdorf." But he also let it be clearly understood that when she ran her household and the farm she really did so only in his name, and that the rights of a wife must remain within certain limits. "In the household I let her be in charge without prejudice to my rights; but in other fields the dominance of a woman has, from the beginning of this world never done any good."[14] He would laughingly call her "my lord and my Moses Käthe," especially when her sense of economy conflicted with his boundless liberality and generosity. (It is a truly remarkable coincidence that for twenty-five years the World Savings Day has been held on the 31st of October!). But he remained boss.

That does not mean that they were accustomed to squabbling. Theirs was a happy marriage, founded in mutual love and esteem. Neither friend nor foe ever reported a real disturbance of peace between these two. Many a foe would have been extremely glad if he had been able to record such dissension—and they were living in a glass house. "Katie, you have a man who loves you," he said. And she did love him. He wrote to a friend: "My Kate is in all things so obliging and pleas-

---

[14]Georg Rietschel, *Luther und sein Haus.* Leipzig, 1917, 42 ff.

ing to me that I would not exchange my poverty for the riches of Croesus."[15] What a faithful husband has to be, he explained thus in a marriage sermon: "You hear how well the Apostle teaches a man to conduct himself towards his wife. He should not consider her a rag on which to wipe his feet; and, indeed, she was not created from a foot but from a rib in the center of man's body, so that the man is to regard her not otherwise than his own body and flesh. . . . And although another woman be prettier, better, wiser, healthier, and more eloquent and prudent than your wife, you should nonetheless not love *her* as much as you love your own body. Nay, nay, *your* wife you should love as your own body. And although she does not always please you, have patience with her as with your own body."[16]

Luther's family life is described at length in all biographies of the reformer, and therefore it is very well known.[17] His was a normal family. There was joy on the occasion of a birth and grief in the case of a death. When his first-born Hans was being firmly wrapped in napkins (as was customary in those days on the occasion of a birth) and violently kicked in protest, Luther looked at him and laughed, "Go on, kick! The pope tried to bind me, but I kicked his fetters off!" And when the little coffin of his beloved daughter Magdalena was nailed down he said, weeping, "Hammer on, she will rise again on the day of judgment!"

A famous letter of Luther's is the one he wrote from the Coburg to his "dearly beloved son Hansel Luther," who was then 4 years old, about the delights of the chil-

---

[15]WA, Br., iv, Nr. 1032 (11-5-1526).
[16]WA, xvii (1), 24 (Eine Predigt vom Ehestand, 1525).
[17]See also: Julius Boehmer, *Luthers Ehebuch.* Zwickau, 1935; and Georg Buchwald, *Martin Luthers als Kind, Vater und Freund,* Berlin, 1957.

67

dren's heaven, full of play and pleasure. From other letters, written later, and from the Table Talks, it appears that Hans was beginning to show the unpleasant characteristics of a spoilt child.[18] A remarkable letter is the one Luther wrote in 1542. Sixteen-year-old Hans had been sent to the headmaster of the Latin school in Torgau for his education. When he had been there a short time, he was called back because his sister was dying. After the funeral he had to go to Torgau again. Then, at Christmas, Hans was not allowed to go home. Luther wrote to the headmaster, "As a result of the death of his sister and especially of the conversations with his mother, my son has become weak-hearted. But he must not give in to his sentiments, and he cannot come home, or he will never become a real man." To Hans he wrote, "Do your best to master your tears like a man, and be careful not to give your mother pain again and not to make her anxious about you; she is always so inclined to worry. You must be obedient to God, and God has entrusted us, your parents, to bring you up and make a man of you. Then you will no longer be a weakling. Mother is not writing you herself, but she has said that you can come home only if you do not feel well. By that she meant of course: if you are really ill you must tell us at once. Further, she wants you to master your sorrow and to study cheerfully and quietly." This letter, more so perhaps than the famous one about the gardens of heaven, testifies to Luther's wise paternal love.

In his sermon *Von dem ehelichen Stand* the reformer deals with the education of children. He says: "There is nothing which will more surely earn hell for a man than the improper training of his children; and parents

---

[18]WA, Br., viii, 19 (to Hans, 27-1-'37); x, 228 (to Markus Crodel, 26-12-'42); x, 229 (to Hans, 27-1-'42).

can perform no more damaging bit of work than to neglect their offspring, to let them curse, swear, learn indecent words and songs, and permit them to live as they please. Some parents themselves incite their children to such sins by giving them superfluous finery and temporal advancement, so that they may but please the world, rise high and become wealthy. They are constantly concerned to provide sufficiently for the body rather than for the soul. . . . But the child will be required from the parent on Judgment Day in a very strict reckoning."[19]

The reformer had more trouble with his nephews and nieces than with his own six children. No fewer than seven children of his sisters and of one of his brothers were either sent to him for their education or received into his family as orphans. Some of the boys and also one of the girls gave him many difficulties. For, as their fosterfather, Luther insisted on giving consent to matrimony, and this was not always to their liking. Secret engagements, in the Catholic Church accepted by canon law even if they were made against the wish of the parents, he did not acknowledge. According to him, the authority of the *paterfamilias* may not be interfered with, not even by the pope and his marriage laws. No child should marry or be married against the will of his or her father, even though that father must not force a husband upon his daughter. These theories at times were the cause of great conflicts in the Luther household. But when a wedding was celebrated with his consent, it was a merry and abundant sort of feast. Luther procured venison through the intermediary of his princely friends. He sampled the wine personally, being a connoisseur him-

---

[19]WA, ii, 170 (Translation by Ewald M. Plass, *This Is Luther*. St. Louis, 1948, 263).

self. No trouble was too great for him then, as he said: "I want to do the right thing by them and so honour my parents, now dead, fulfill their will, and be a help to the children of ungrateful people."[20]

But the limit had not yet been reached with the five children of his own and the seven foster-children. There were also some schoolteachers in the Black Monastery for the education of the children, sometimes with a few extra pupils of their own. Then a number of students stayed with the Luthers, paying (or not paying) a moderate sum for their board. They were a regular feature of any professor's household in those days. The number of guests staying for a short time was endless. Fugitive monks and nuns, banned evangelical preachers, children of colleagues who had died of the plague, friends and scholars from elsewhere—it was a perpetual come-and-go in this hospitable house. Fortunately, Mrs. Luther was assisted not only by maid-servants and man-servants but also by an aunt, some grand-nieces and other female inmates; and the "Morningstar of Wittenberg" was a thrifty housewife. She possessed the virtue of domesticity and she was in her element when she managed a large household.

When Prince George of Anhalt wanted to visit Wittenberg and considered the idea of staying with Luther, one of his friends wrote him, "The house of Luther is occupied by a motley crowd of boys, students, girls, widows, old women and youngsters. For this reason there is much disturbance in the place and many regret it for the sake of the good man, the honorable father. If but the spirit of Doctor Luther lived in all of these, his house would offer you an agreeable, friendly quarter for a few days, so that Your Grace would be able to enjoy the

---

[20]WA, T., i, Nr. 1108 (1530-35); ii, Nr. 2346 (1531).

hospitality of that man. But as the situation now stands and as circumstances exist in the household of Luther, I would not advise that Your Grace stop there."[21]

A man with a busy and hectic life such as Luther's must at times have been driven almost crazy in such an overcrowded house. Not even in his study in the tower was he always safe. In 1537 the Electress of Brandenburg lay ill in his house. Her daughter, the Princess of Anhalt, visited her and also wanted to see the reformer. The latter did not feel too well, and besides, did not like this woman because she was not a good wife to her husband. So he remained in his study. All the same, after dinner the Princess entered his cell without being announced. But she was sharply censured in these words: "People of your standing should set an example of manners," snapped Luther at her.[22]

On the whole, though, this busy life does not seem to have hindered him. "King Solomon fed 24,000 people every day," he said, "and all the poor relations from his father's house came to stay in the palace, just as happens here in the Black Monastery. That's why that king needed so many wives. They were all of them kept pretty busy."[23]

Katharina looked after and prepared the meals over which Luther himself presided. To the latter fact we owe the extensive collection of Table Talks, which form an inexhaustible source of information about himself and his environment. There were days when Luther did not feel like talking at table and practiced a "monastic silence." But usually he started the conversation after

[21]Theodor Kolde, *Analecta Lutherana*. Gotha, 1883, 378 (Translation by E. G. Schwiebert, *Luther and His Times*. St. Louis, 1950, 597).

[22]Julius Köstlin, a.a.O., 511.

[23]Ernst Kroker, *Katharina von Bora, Luthers Frau*. Zwickau, 1925, 147.

grace by asking his guests if there was any news. Then he discussed the things that occupied him in connection with his literary work and his correspondence. He often told stories from his own life, especially from his days of struggle. Not all stories, though, appear to have tallied with history!

In 1531, one his students, Conrad Cordatus, began very discreetly to make notes of these talks. When it appeared that Luther did not object to this, others followed suit. The notebooks were passed round among the students, were copied and added to. All together there are 6,596 entries. Not all that was taken down is important for us, nor is everything original. The language is a mixture of German and Latin, which is what was spoken at table. Many sayings in German, however, were taken down in Latin, because the theological students had their own shorthand system in that language. Johann Aurifaber, who during the last few years of Luther's life lived with him and was his assistant, arranged as many as 3000 of these table talks under 80 different headings, and published them in 1566, with the motto he took from John 6:12, "Gather up the fragments that are left." These Table Talks were given in the last 15 years of Luther's life. What we find in them about the monk Martinus and the young professor Luther is colored by retrospection. They are the memories of an aging man making his own mental picture of the days of his young manhood, with a tendency to add a little extra color here and there. A wonderful collection of anecdotes and wisdom of life, it has to be used with care by those wanting to find scholarly facts.

In his large family Luther acted as a house priest. In the popular and witty booklet he wrote in 1533, "A simple way of praying for a good friend," he points out that a family father is instructed by God to lead his family in prayer.[24] That is the basis of all education. Wherever that is neglected the home becomes a pigsty and an institute for the instruction of rascals, he says. He himself gave the example. Every morning, with his children, he said the Ten Commandments, the Creed, the Lord's Prayer and a psalm. He, too, needed that. "I have never risen above the children's lessons, every day I have to learn to understand them. I, the great doctor, still receive the same instruction as my children." Before dinner he read a portion of the Bible, which he often discussed during the meal. After dinner he led the singing of the Latin responses of the church year, and of old religious songs and chorales. His own wonderful Christmas hymn for children. "Vom Himmel hoch da komm ich her" ("From heav'n above to earth I come") almost certainly was composed in the family circle and was dramatized there by the whole family. In the evening a lot of games were played by the whole family, such as ninepins, chess and various card games. From them Luther took so many illustrations for his theological theories that they could be the subject of quite a lengthy essay.

Once a year a catechism examination was held. The children and the younger housemates had to say portions from the catechism and from the Gospels, and had to sing psalms. At one time, when this was done very timidly, Luther reminded the candidate of the day of judgment, when all of us will have to render account of our faith publicly. The exam was followed by a festive meal and students performed a comedy by Terentius, Luther's favorite comedy-writer. After the feast (called *Königreich* or *regnum,* kingdom) Luther usually had long

---

[24]WA, xxxviii, 358-375.

talks with his friends, such as Melanchthon, Bugenhagen and others, till his wife came in, played the role of the boss of the house, and made an end of it.

Finally we come to his *Hauspredigten*, family sermons. Whenever our reformer, who for years also served as minister for the town (some 2000 sermons have been preserved), did not feel well, he preached for his family and the servants. Justus Jonas once asked him why he did that. People are not that keen on hearing the word of God, he said. Luther answered, "If I cannot preach in a church I preach in my home, because of the office I hold and for my conscience, simply because as a family father it is my duty to preach to my family.[25] On those occasions he preached as simply as he could. As for that, it is remarkable that in his later years Luther began to explain the Gospel in an ever more simple way, free from any abstruse theological theories. If we want to know what his family sermons were like we should not judge by the so-called *Hauspostille* which were edited by his assistant Veit Dietrich, for those were revised, altered and expanded. We should rather read these sermons in their original version, which, fortunately, has been preserved.

Up to the end Luther remained a dutiful family father. At times he longed for rest and quiet. Then he went to his swine-herd Johannes and talked to him, for he could not keep to himself. "The thing I should like to do most, now that I am getting on in years, is to withdraw from people and to enjoy myself in the garden among the wonders of God, the flowers and the birds." That is what he wrote to Justus Jonas, "but," he goes on, "I realize that I have to carry the burden laid on us by our sins." In the pluralistic office a Christian has in life, especially

---

[25]WA, T., ii, Nr. 2726b (1532).

in his family life, he has to serve his neighbor. That is the task assigned to him by God, giving much that is joyful and much that is good, but at the same time teaching man, if he is selfish and ease-loving, how he must mortify the flesh by serving and loving his neighbor. Then he will find the Cross that kills the old man and gives life to the new man, born in Jesus Christ the Lord.[26]

---

[26]Gustaf Wingren, a.a.O., 48 f.

Luther as He Saw Himself

WHEN the 26-year old brother Martinus was asked by the vicar-general of the Augustinian order in Wittenberg to take a doctor's degree in theology and to take over the latter's chair in biblical exegesis, Luther had no fewer than fifteen objections. Not because he thought a monk should be humble, but he really found it a very heavy task. One of his objections was: It is a waste of energy and money, because such a thing would probably be the death of me. Von Staupitzen's answer is well-known: That doesn't matter much; God in heaven can use doctors of theology as His advisers, for He is extremely busy.

For the time being the young doctor would have enough to do serving his God in this world. This monk who preferred the quiet of his study was called out of his cell to play a prominent part amongst popes and monarchs, princes and prelates on the stage of world history. Against his own will he was gradually put in the forefront, till he found himself in the bright footlights.

Ordered by his superior, he took the oath on the Holy Scripture, and this gave him the strength in days of doubt to continue. "I, doctor Martin Luther, have been called and forced to take this doctor's degree. Against my own will, merely out of obedience, I have done this. Then I had to take the chair, and I swore and promised on the Holy Scriptures, so dear to me, to preach and teach the Word of God truly and purely. When I was doing that, the pope objected and tried to stop me. He did not have much success, as you know; he will have less and less of it and he will not be able to stop me. In the name of God and my vocation I want to tread on lions and snakes."[1]

The calling to the chair of Biblical exegesis was indeed the cause of the whole chain of events which, *nolens volens,* was to leave him on the spot where God wanted him to be. His zeal to understand the Bible was the ardor of a man who is looking for help in his spiritual distress, for peace with God. And while explaining the Bible professionally and at the same time personally, he rediscovered the heart of the Gospel, the justification of the sinner by faith alone.

The posting of the 95 theses against the indulgences can hardly be considered as a public action. That was within the sphere of university life, and Luther thought that he said something that every religious person would agree with. In those days he was far from convinced that he was the man to come forward as a reformer. "The church does need a reformation," he writes in his *Resolutiones,* an explanation of the theses, "but that is not the work for a human being, nor for one pope or many cardinals, as it was thought at the last two councils—that

---

[1]WA, xxx (3), 386 (Glosse auf das vermeinte kaiserliche Edikt, 1531).

is the task of the whole world, yea and more, it is God's work."[2]

But if it should appear that God could use him as an instrument, he would be willing, though frightened. To his friend Lang he wrote: "I do not want the things I am doing to be completed by human activity and understanding. Only God's activity and plan count. If it is God's work, who is going to stop it? And if it is not God's work, who will be able to further it? Not my will, not theirs, not ours, but Thy will be done, our Father who art in heaven. Amen."[3]

The real push was given the next year by Cardinal Cajetan, and by Professor Eck the year after. The resistance and hatred he met with convinced him that he was on the correct way, that he preached the right doctrine. "For this is the best proof that a doctrine is right, if the mass and the high ones and the wise ones feel insulted."[4] But not for a moment did he think himself able to achieve a reformation of the church. A reformation is not a human achievement; it would be ridiculous if a human being should decide to accomplish it.

That, really, is the difference between Luther and various other persons of the later middle ages who in their apocalyptical expectations dream of a renewal of the original pure status of Christianity and feel themselves called upon to reorganize the Church of Christ.[5] Luther distinguishes himself from them in the sober way in which he sees that history is God's work, and he is

[2]WA, i, 627 (Resolutiones disputationum de indulgentiarum virtute, 1518).
[3]WA, Br., i, 122 (to Johann Lang, 11-11-1517).
[4]WA, Br., ii, 110 (to Heinrich von Bünau, 30-5-1520).
[5]Wilhelm Maurer, "Was verstand Luther unter Reformation der Kirche?" in Luther, Mitt. der Luthergesellsch., 1957, 54-57.

afraid to obstruct the Lord. He wants to leave it to God alone to choose the way He wishes him to go.

When the Wittenberg professor went to Worms, many people hoped that he would be the man, the great restorer who was going to start the work. He was surrounded by high-strung expectations. Michael Stifel, an apocalyptic man, prophesied that the monk from Wittenberg was the angel who, as it says in Revelation (14:6), flies in the midst of heaven, having the everlasting Gospel, announcing the future fall of the whore of Babylon. And even Melanchthon called him *Elia Redivivus*, percursor of the returning Christ. But Luther rejected such qualifications. He did not want to be a prophet except in the sense of a preacher of God's Word. "I am sure that I possess God's Word and that I have been called as His preacher. But I am afraid to bring about a new order."[6] This bond with the Word defined his attitude in Worms, made him conquer his hesitation, and still safeguarded him from bravado.

One of his latest German biographers, Karl August Meissinger, says that Luther during the days in Worms missed his best chance to take up the leadership over the German Empire. In a very tragic way, Meissinger says, the reformer did not come up to expectations.[7] However, this assertion is erroneous. Luther did not want to be a "German prophet" in this way. I admit, sometimes he called himself a "prophet of the Germans,"[8] but he meant by this that he had to criticize and warn his countrymen on the strength of God's Word. It is his attitude towards the Word that matters, not his

---

[6]WA, xi, 210 (Sermon, 1523).

[7]K. A. Meissinger, *Luther. Die deutsche Tragödie, 1521.* Bern, 1953. 184 f.

[8]WA, xxx (2), 588 (Eine Predigt dass man Kinder zu Schule halten soll, 1530); xxx (3), 290 (Warnung an seine lieben Deutschen, 1531).

prophetic vocation or self-consciousness. "I do not call myself a prophet," he wrote in the decisive year 1521, "but I say that my enemies should be afraid of my being one according as they despise me and respect themselves. . . . Even if I am not a prophet, I am sure that I possess God's Word and that they do not."[9] And, later, too, that was what he stuck to. He felt himself an apostle more than a prophet. Special revelations were not conferred upon him, and a particular calling did not come to him. "Christ alone is the prophet we should listen to."[10] "I have one prophecy, namely that God's Word is the truth."[11]

His stay at the Wartburg was of great importance for the development of Luther's self-assurance as a reformer. In his hours of solitude he became convinced that, acting the part of a leader, he was held responsible for the continuance of the preaching of the Gospel. This became apparent when, through the actions of the Enthusiasts, the leadership almost got into the wrong hands. The letters, so filled with grandeur, which he wrote to the Elector on his return express this very strikingly. He realized that he was doing something extremely dangerous but felt himself unassailable in his vocation. "Your Grace knows (and if you do not know may you be herewith informed) that I have received the Gospel not from human beings but from our Lord Jesus Christ, and for this reason I may boast of being a servant and an evangelist, and from now on that is what I want to call myself."[12]

In his famous Invocavit-sermons, delivered during the

<hr />

[9]WA, vii, 313 (Grund und Ursach aller Artikel D. Martin Luthers, 1521).
[10]WA, T., v, Nr. 6409.
[11]WA, T., i, Nr. 1125 (1530-35).
[12]WA, Br., ii, 455 (5-3-1522).

first week after his return to Wittenberg, sermons in which he stresses the responsibility of every faithful person towards God, he begs his congregation to listen to him: "Dear brothers, follow me. I cannot be wrong. I am the first person whom God has used as an instrument for this plan. I have been the first man to whom God revealed the preaching of His Word."[13]

Looking back on these decisive years, one has to admit that Luther spoke the truth when he said that he was not after the position of reformer. He had no such intentions. "I confess that I did not start all this intentionally, it all happened *divino consilio,* by God's decision."[14] He had no idea beforehand of how deep the contrasts were, what fierce battles his preaching was to cause. "I would not have had the courage to attack and incense the pope and the whole world. God has put me here as a horse with blinkers."[15]

Luther realized only afterwards what the issues had been. The explanation is not so much to be looked for in his psychological nature[16] as in his theological doctrine.[17] He was convinced that God's work is done in secret; it is a hidden work. It cannot be planned and calculated. God makes use of human beings and their considerations, but often He does so by counteracting them. He uses His servants as His instruments, many times against their will and in such a way that they do not know how. Luther liked to cite Moses, whom God

---

[13]WA, x (3), 8.
[14]WA, T., iv, Nr. 3944 (5-8-1538)
[15]WA, T., iii, Nr. 3846 (1538).
[16]Cf. W. Walther, *Luther Charakter,* Leipzig, 1917.[2]
[17]Cf. Karl Holl, "Luthers Urteile über sich selbst," in *Ges. Aufsätze zur Kirchengesch.,* I, *Luther,* 1932[6], 381-419; Hans Frhr. von Campenhausen, "Reformatorisches Selbstbewusstsein und reformatorisches Geschichtsbewusstsein bei Luther (1517-1522)," in *Archiv für Reformationsgesch.,* 37 (1940), 128-150.

at first passed by (Ex. 33:23) as an example. "Thou shalt not see my face, the Lord says, thou shalt not know my plans, but thou shalt see me from behind. Afterwards thou shalt know what I have done, not before." This Luther applied to his own life. Only afterwards he realized that God wanted to use him in the work of the reformation.

"Who would ever have imagined that such an opposition against the pope would arise in Germany?" he asks.[18] He certainly did not. God kept the plan He had made for Martin Luther a secret from him a long time.

Of course, all this has its psychological side too. Luther was naturally a modest man. He had no need to assert himself and was not a leader by nature. When somebody was guided by ambition, he was convinced that that person was tempted by the devil. Against his will, against his nature did he take this position of leadership. "If I had known beforehand it would not have been easy for God to get me this far. But since I started this with Him I want to make it a success. Not for the world should I ever do this again. I would not dare to take such a terribly great and heavy responsibility and fear upon me. But, on the other hand, when I look up to Him who called me to do this, I am glad I did not refuse."[19]

But as he was convinced that God had put him on the road to the reformation he stressed again and again that God was responsible for the progress and that the result was up to Him. "I have placed myself at His disposal and surrendered to Him in the name of the Lord. His will be done. Who asked Him to make me a doctor? Why, once He had done so, He will have His way, other-

[18] WA, T., v, Nr. 5536 (1542-43).
[19] WA, T., i, Nr. 113 (1531).

wise He had better cancel it, if He regrets having let me take my doctor's degree."[20] Another quotation: "I have repeated so many times, if it is God's will that I started, nobody can undo it. If it is not God's will, somebody else will have to go on, I will not do so. I have nothing to lose, because I did not stake anything. But I know that nobody can take it from me, only God."[21]

In this respect as well, scholars have tried to distinguish between the younger and the older Luther, between the ardent hero of faith and the retrospective, disappointed old man. Of course, there is a difference, as there always will be between a man in the strength of his life and an elderly man. When in his later years Luther looked back on the critical period in his life, he could hardly imagine that he had had the incomprehensible courage to do such a risky thing, and he was the more convinced that he himself did not complete it. "God can make a man so foolhardy, but I do not know if I would be as mad again."[22]

There is another difference: before 1525 he stressed the dispensability of his person: God can make many *doctores Martinos*. If I am not worth it, He will use somebody else as His instrument.[23] Later he realized that, in spite of all, God had done it through him. At that time he could talk about the historical importance of his person in a remarkably objective way. He talked about it as if discussing somebody else, so much did he look at things from a distance. It was only the thing itself that was all-important.

But through the years he stuck to his conviction that

[20]WA, Br., i, 611 (to Spalatinus, 14-1-1520).
[21]WA, xviii, 134 (Wider die himmlischen Propheten, 1525).
[22]WA, T., v, Nr. 5342b, 69, 20 f. (1540).
[23]WA, Br., i, 352 (to Spalatinus, 24-2-1519); ii, 128 (to Spalatinus, 10-7-1520).

Martin Luther was only an instrument in the hands of the almighty God. It was not he who revealed the Word but the Word revealed itself; the living Word as a personified power, i.e., Christ Himself, went His own way. This Word took its servant and sent him out and maintained him in the midst of all kinds of dangers. The Gospel revealed itself again in this decisive hour of world history and made this an hour of the history of grace. There is no reason at all, Luther says, to praise the person who preached this Gospel. Does not God always make use of that which is simple and despised to reveal Himself? Did not He preach once by means of an ass?

Thus he could say to his congregation, in the midst of the turbulence of the enthusiasts who thought they could promote God's work with their zeal, "I have only preached, proclaimed and written God's Word. I have not done anything else. While I was sleeping, or drinking Wittenberg beer with my friends Philippus and Amsdorf, this Word did more to weaken the papacy than any sovereign or emperor has ever harmed it. I have not done anything. The Word alone has done and completed everything. . . . I have let the Word work."[24] And 15 years later he still thought in the same way. "We cast all our burdens upon the Lord, we want to make Him responsible, it is His business. He will make it a success. We want to eat, drink, sleep."[25]

This is the reason why Luther was never able to become a religious-political agitator like Zwingli, or an ecclesiastical organizer like Calvin. He realized this himself. His vocation was not a political or a social one, his duty was to preach the Gospel. As he says himself, he was too softhearted and credulous to be a good or-

[24]WA, x (3), 18 (Invocavit-sermon, 1522).
[25]WA, T., iii, Nr. 3518 (1537).

84

ganizer. Maybe, he said, he could get over this, but nevertheless he was not a good governor by nature. "I do not like to rule, I do not have it in me."[26]

It is one of the most remarkable proofs of Luther's self-knowledge that he seldom tried to interfere in public affairs. But ultimately this sometimes passive attitude was determined by his theological ideas. The Word of God does its work, we can let it take its own course. A preacher of the Gospel does his duty, he does not know the results, he leaves it to God. "It is God's business, His care, it is God's work, His victory and glory. He will fight and conquer, without us," he writes to his friend Nicolaus Gerbel.[27] When Luther says such a thing it is more than just a phrase.

Luther did not really expect any important political results from the reformation. For him the expectations of martyrdom and of the return of Christ were too important to allow him to be bothered with politics. In this respect he was the same in his younger and later years, though these expectations became deeper and more profound through the years. As an elderly man he saw God's ordeal coming to the wicked people of Wittenberg, of Germany, and of the world. He said that for his sake, because of his prayers, God would keep back His punishments as long as His servant would live. But "when I am dead it will come."[28] And how he was longing for the blessed hour and looking forward to the good, great day of Christ!

Besides all this, during his whole life he was pursued and oppressed by what he called his *Anfechtungen*, temptations by the devil. Heinrich Boehmer's idea, namely

---

[26]WA, T., v, Nr. 5284 (3-10-1540); Nr. 5538 (1542-43).
[27]WA, Br., iii, 404 (to Nik. Gerbel, 17-12-1524).
[28]WA, T., iii, Nr. 3429. Cf. Hans Preuss, *Martin Luther der Deutsche.* Gütersloh, 1934, 98.

that these *Anfechtungen* in Luther's young manhood were connected only with his struggle for faith, and that in later years they had a more physical character, especially bearing upon his anxiety about his work,[29] was rightly disproved by Roland Bainton.[30] In the *Anfechtungen* throughout the years everything turns on the struggle for faith. There is a slight difference of stress. During the first years this question oppressed him: "Are you the only wise one? Have all theologians up to now been wrong?"[31] And in his dark hours he "entertained thoughts about his being the only person in the world picked out by the devil for special attention."[32] Later he did not worry about himself so much, but sometimes he was anxious about the Christians whom he would have misled and ruined if he had not spoken the truth and had been a false teacher.[33]

The biggest temptation that followed him all his life was whether or not God really wanted to accept and use his work. But there is only one way out: he puts everything up to God. "I cannot say that I am right and wise, and that the others are wrong and unwise, so that I would have to win for that reason. But then I go into my cell, I pray and sigh without anybody noticing and throw the key at God's feet, saying: Good Lord, it is your business and not mine. From the beginning of the world till now you have maintained it without me and you can maintain it till eternity without me. . . . Thus I put my heavenly rights on the shoulders of our Lord

[29]Heinrich Boehmer, *Road to Reformation*. Philadelphia, 1946, 93.

[30]*Church History* 16 (1947), 167-176. Cf. Heinrich Boehmer, *Der junge Luther, mit einem Nachwort von Heinrich Bornhamm*, 1951, 368 f.

[31]WA, ii, 403 (Resolutiones Lutherianae super propositionibus suis Lipsiae disputatis, 1519); viii, 483 (Vom Missbrauch der Messe, 1521).

[32]Albert Hyma, *New Light on Martin Luther*. Grand Rapids, 1958, 113.

[33]WA, T., i, Nr. 141 (1531); Nr. 571 (1533); Nr. 612 (1533).

and I leave it to Him. He can look after things better than I can. He will find the ways and means, as He has always done, does now and will do, I am sure."[34] Psychologically speaking Luther belongs to the cyclothyme type. He was a man whose moods changed very quickly. Periods of depression and of happiness followed each other in a large scale of hyperthyme and hypothyme moments. The latest researches in this field[35] have made it clear that in Luther's case one cannot speak of a pathological structure, of a manic-depressive psychosis, as some scholars used to do.[36] On the contrary, this large scale of moods in his character was of enormous positive importance for his work. He needed both the days of depression and the times of happy zeal for his work, and almost exuberant courage to fight against his adversaries. As he says he needed temptations as much as meat and drink, and on the other hand he could get on with his work best when his blood was boiling with indignation. To put it in a theological way: Does not God lead those whom He uses always through the depths, and then upward again? "First there is an extreme weakness and an endless despair, so that the mind does not know where to look for help and advice. But whenever God really helps, it goes beyond prayers and understanding."[37]

With this psychological structure goes the fact that Luther, especially in his later years, could be very rude, harsh and uncompromising in his rage.[38] That, too, he

[34]WA, liii, 660 (Der 101. Psalm ausgelegt, 1534).

[35]Eberhard Grossmann, *Beiträge zur psychologischen Analyse der Reformatoren Luther und Calvin*. Basel-New York, 1958.

[36]Cf. P. J. Reiter, *Martin Luthers Umwelt, Carakter, Psychose*, I-II. Kopenhagen, 1937-1941.

[37]WA, xxv, 380 (Lecture on Isaiah, 1527-1529).

[38]Cf. Kurt Ihlenfeld, "Luther als Polemiker," in *Luther, Mitt. der Lutherges*. 1955, 35-45.

knew himself. He calls himself a *homo iracundus*[39] and he knew that he was often driven by a fierceness and fought with rough weapons. He was not ashamed of this. "I may be a little unmannerly at times but I am open and sincere, and in this respect better than my adversaries."[40] In his speaking and writing he was always completely honest with himself and embarrassingly frank with friend and foe. Many of his utterances are very candid, without being candied at all. Candor is just a different thing from candy. Luther always meant what he said and wrote, and he rarely failed to say and write all he meant. That biographers—especially the Roman Catholic—can stress the rudeness in the character of the reformer, they owe to his openness and his honesty. He wore his heart on his sleeve,[41] and thus supplied his critics with a large stock of quotations.

"Before God and His dear Christians" he would admit that he often went too far, being a weak man and a sinner who had no reason to boast of anything. But the world and the unbelievers will know that "they are not worthy to undo his strap."[42] "I know that the faithful must be humble, but before the pope I will be proud with a holy pride."[43] For what reason? Because he understood the Scriptures better than any sophist or papist.

That the Bible came first with Luther is proved by the fact that he did not attach much importance to his own writings. They only served to guide the people to the real source. Once they had done so, they could dis-

---

[39]WA, xliii, 46 (Lecture on Genesis, 1535-1545). Cf. WA, T., i, Nr. 197; iii, Nr. 2836.

[40]WA, Br., ii, 45 (to Spalatinus, 16-2-1520).

[41]Cf. Ewald M. Plass, *This Is Luther*. St. Louis, 1948, 212-242.

[42]WA, xxiii, 29 (Auf des Königs zu England Lästerschrift Antwort, 1527).

[43]WA, xl (1), 180 (Lecture on Galatians, 1531).

appear.[44] With this view goes the fact that Luther did not write books, he wrote only pamphlets and tracts, though some of them are rather bulky and their number is very large. He did not even know all the titles himself. It was left to his friends to make a catalogue[45] and to advance a complete edition of his works. Luther himself, on their instance, wrote the prefaces to these publications. But he did it in his own way.

In the preface to the collection of his Latin works (1545) he wrote:

I have long and earnestly resisted those who wished that my books, or rather the confused mass of my lucubrations, should be published, both because I was unwilling that the labors of the ancients should be overwhelmed by my novelties, and that my readers should be hindered from reading them, and because now, through God's grace, there are a great number of methodical books—among which Philip's *Commonplaces* excel—whereby a divine and a bishop may be well and amply trained to be mighty in preaching the doctrine of godliness; more especially since the Holy Bible itself may now be had in almost every language, while my own books, as the disorderly course of events led, or rather compelled me, are themselves a sort of rude, undigested chaos, which I myself should now find it difficult to arrange. For these reasons I wished that all my books were buried in perpetual oblivion that there might be room for better ones.[46]

And at the end of the preface to the collection of his German works (1539) he wrote:

If you feel and fancy that you really have what it takes to be successful and are tickled about your own booklets, teachings and writings, as though you have done splendidly and have preached excellently well, are also greatly pleased

[44]Cf. Karl Holl, a.a.O., 398 f.
[45]WA, xxxviii, 133 (Vorrede zum Catalogus oder Register aller Bücher und Schriften Luthers, 1533).
[46]WA, liv, 179 (Translation by Plass, *op. cit.*, 203 f.).

that you are praised before others, perhaps also desire to be praised or you would mourn and quit—if you are of that stripe, dear friend, take hold of your ears, and if you grasp aright you will find a pair of large, long, rough ass's ears. Moreover, you ought then to assume the expense of adorning them with golden bells so that, wherever you go, one may hear you, point the finger at you, and say: "See! See! There goes the fine animal that can write such splendid books and can preach so excellently!" Then you will be blessed and superblessed in the kingdom of heaven—yea, where hell fire has been prepared for the devil and his angels![47]

That Luther was a humble man by nature also appears from this that he valued some of his friends as theologians and reformers more highly than he did himself. In his opinion men like Brenz, Amsdorf, and Bugenhagen possessed the qualities he did not have. He suggested that not only Melanchthon but Caspar Cruciger as well would appear to be the real reformers, and that it would become evident that he had been only their precursor.[48] Indeed, he did not think much of himself at all. When an old man, he described himself and his work in the following manner: "A miserable member of the staff of the high and real Judge, who has had during almost 30 years his seat near the door of the chancery and who served a few times as an errand-boy or postman."[49] He wrote this to the archbishop of Mainz, his chief. And he continued: "Nevertheless, sitting at the door in God's Chancery, I overheard that in heaven they don't think too much of you!"

The remarkable tension between Luther's humility and his self-consciousness as a reformer manifests itself most clearly in his attitude with respect to the use of his

---

[47]WA, 1, 660 (Translation by Plass, *op. cit.*, 204).

[48]WA, Br., ii, 167 (to Johann Lang, 18-8-1520); vii, 329 (to Nikolaus Gerbel, 27-11-1535).

[49]WA, l, 399 (Wider den Bischof zu Magdeburg, Albrecht Kardinal, 1539).

name for his followers. Soon the followers of Luther were called Lutherans. Their adversaries, Eck and Emser, had invented this appellation as a nickname for the new heretics, and soon it was used generally. Luther resisted strongly. As early as 1522 he wrote:

"I beg you not to use my name and not to call yourselves Lutherans but Christians. What is Luther? The doctrine is not mine. I have not been crucified for anybody. . . . How could I, stinking bag of maggots, allow the children of Christ to be called by my no-good name? Do not do this, my dear friends. We should forget about such party-names and call ourselves Christians, because it is He who taught us. . . . I am nobody's master and do not not want to be. I, and with me the whole church, possess the only doctrine of Christ who alone is our Master."[50]

He feared lest his followers should establish a new "order," a sort of "order of the Lutherans"; he, on the contrary, hoped that the entire church of Christ, the "one order of Christianity," would be reformed through the Holy Ghost.[51]

In a letter to Ritter Hartmut von Cronberg Luther says that many people believe because of him, but the only persons who have real faith are those who would stick to it, even if they heard—which heaven may forbid—that Luther himself had denied his own doctrine. "For such persons do not believe in Luther, but in Christ Himself. The Word possesses them and they possess the Word. They do not need to care about Luther, whether he is a rascal or a saint. I myself do not know any Luther, do not want to know him either. I do not preach anything from him, only the Word of Christ. The devil may take Luther to hell, if he can."[52]

---

[50]WA, viii, 685 (Eine treue Vermahnung zu allen Christen, 1522).
[51]WA, l, 272 (Die drei Symbola, 1538).
[52]WA, x, (2), 58 (Eine Missive an Hartmut von Cronberg, 1522).

3716+

Typical of his attitude in this respect is what happened during the Diet of Augsburg. Melanchthon had written to Luther, then staying on the Coburg, concerning a certain decision the Evangelicals made in Augsburg: "We have acted upon your authority." And Luther replied—though he did not hide his opinion about Melanchthon's weak guidance in Augsburg and though he really did assert his power from the Coburg—in these words: "I do not want to be an authority and prefer not to be called so in this matter. Though you can make this word acceptable, I do not want to hear it. If it is not your business just as much as it is mine, I do not want it to be called mine, as if I had driven it through."[53]

I must end now. Though I have already cited the reformer himself many times—are not quotations the best part of all books and lectures about Luther?—I still want to conclude with another citation. It is taken from that most remarkable document which he drew up in 1542, his last will. It is more than a summary of his inheritance; it is at the same time a testimony of the way he saw himself. With a very curious self-consciousness he looked back at his work as a reformer. He did not want to involve a notary in this testament. That his signature had to be legalized he thought unnecessary. He wrote:

"Let me be the person I really am, known in heaven and on earth as well as in hell . . . because God, the Father of all mercy, has entrusted me, poor, damned, unworthy, miserable sinner, with the Gospel of His beloved Son, has saved me and found me a faithful and truthful witness thus far, so that many people all over the world have accepted the Gospel through me and consider me as teacher of the truth, in spite of the excommunication by the pope and the rage of emperors and princes, of rulers and priests, yea, of all the devils."

[53]WA, Br., v, 406 (29-6-1530).

And he called himself "God's notary and witness in His Gospel: Martin Luther."[54]

At the end of his life Luther often felt too tired and weary to give any lectures in the University. "*Volo esse miles emeritus,* I would like to go on a long furlough," he sighed. His friends urged him to continue his work. Were not they always among his audience? Then he replied: "I will go on for a while, but not because of you. I only do it for the sake of the freshmen, so that later they can say: Once I used to go to Luther's lectures."[55] But that, of course, is not to be taken seriously. For he knew that it was not his doctrine but the Gospel of Christ they needed[56] and he also said: "I do not want to hear: 'Doctor Martin Luther has taught me this or that.' But rather say: 'I believe in God the Father, the Son and the Holy Ghost.' "[57] And after all he is quite sure that God, in the day of judgment, will say to him:"*Tu bene docuisti!* You taught [my Gospel] in the right way."[58]

---

[54]WA, Br., ix, 573 f. Cf. E. A. Doleschall, *Luthers Testament.* Budapest, 1881.

[55]Hans von Schubert, *Zu Luthers Vorlesungstätigkeit* (Sitzungsberichte der Heidelberger Akademie der Wissensch., Philos.-hist. Klasse), 1920, 21.

[56]WA, x (2), 23 (Von beider Gestalt des Sakraments zu nehmen, 1522).

[57]WA, xlix, 684 (Sermon, 18-1-1545).

[58]WA, xvii, 232 (Sermon, 12-5-1525).

Luther at the End of His Days

THE aging Luther was in poor health. With advancing years he complained not only about the ailment from which he had already been suffering for a long time, persistent constipation, but also about singing in the ears and dizziness. Moreover, kidney stones, which once had almost brought him to his grave, continued to trouble him. But worst of all were the recurring spells of oppression in the cardiac region, which were caused by arteriosclerosis of the coronary artery.

The cause of these diseases must be sought in two kinds of circumstances. First we must take into account the excessive way of living in those times. Much eating and drinking was considered to be a sign of health. And though Luther, as Melanchthon informs us, knew times, especially when he worked to capacity all day, in which he contented himself with very little food and when only a herring or two and some bread would do for him, particularly in his later years, he must have eaten and drunk —on the whole—more than is desirable for an elderly man.

The second circumstance is that by the enormous amount of work which he had to get through regularly, he was compelled to a sedentary life. Being constantly overburdened with work, he had not enough opportunity to indulge in recreation, and the almost unbearable responsibility in town and country, in church and society, deprived him of all possibilities for real relaxation.

"Thoughts and work can make a man old," he said ruefully at table one day.[1] And: "When they do a postmortem on me, they will find a small heart, shrunken by all the disappointments which have been my lot."[2]

For more than ten years he had the task of explaining the first book of Moses to his students. Though he himself was often dissatisfied with it, this commentary is full of important theological opinions and original wisdom of life.[3] On the 17th of November 1545 he finished his Genesis lectures. This is the last text of that book: "Thus Joseph died, 110 years old. And they embalmed him and laid him down in a coffin in Egypt." "It was not even of importance to Joseph," Luther said, "where he would be buried, but to bear testimony to his faith in Christ, he wished his bones to be taken to Canaan, the promised land, as a symbol for posterity, that they might continue in the faith in which he and his forefathers had departed this life." And then he concludes his lecture in German: "That was the dear book of Genesis. May the Lord grant that others after me shall do better. I am done up. I am infirm. Pray God for me that He may grant me a good, blessed end."[4]

---

[1]WA, T., iii, Nr. 3843 (19-4-1538)

[2]Julius Köstlin, *Martin Luther*. Berlin, 1903, II, 513. Cf. Erwin Mülhaupt, "Luthers Kampf mit der Krankheit" in *Luther, Mitteilungen der Luthergesellsch.*, 1958, 115-123.

[3]Peter Meinhold, *Die Genesisvorlesung Luthers und ihre Herausgeber.* Stuttgart, 1936.

[4]WA, xliv, 824 f.

Just as Joseph died in a foreign country, Luther was to die outside Wittenberg, where he accomplished his life work and where presently, with great ceremony, his dead body was to be taken. Yet for him it was not "in a foreign country," for he died, by a remarkable coincidence, in his birthplace, in the city of Eisleben. In the county of Mansfeld, from which he came (Luther continued to refer to it as his "native country"), a violent dispute about financial and economic affairs had risen in the family of the counts of Mansfeld after the division of a legacy. In the course of time the rights of the citizens from Eisleben had also been violated. The matter had developed into an intricate knot of civil law questions. Legal advisers had not been able to solve the problem, and law suits increased embitterment. Decay of social and economic life was the consequence of it.

As early as 1540 and 1542 Luther had proposed to intercede and exhorted the factions to settle the dispute. Finally Count Albrecht of Mansfeld requested him to act as an intermediary and Luther's elector permitted him to do so.

In spite of the bad condition of his health, the reformer took this difficult task upon him, for the sake of his " beloved, gracious sovereign lords" and the citizens of his birthplace. In October 1545 he had visited Mansfeld, together with Melanchthon and Justus Jonas, the superintendent of Halle, to settle things. He stayed there over Christmas at the court of the counts, but then he had to go back home owing to illness of Melanchthon, before the affairs had been arranged properly.

At the beginning of the new year the matter was to be discussed definitely at Eisleben. On the 17th of January 1546 Luther preached at Wittenberg for the last time. During these days he also began work on a controversial writing against the Roman Catholic theologians of the universities of Paris and Louvain. From a letter to his old friend Jakob Probst in Bremen we know how he felt.

Old, worn out, infirm, tired, cold and in addition one-eyed, I am writing to you, my Jacobus. I had hoped that now at last the rest, which, as it seems to me, I have sufficiently deserved, would have been granted to me. But it surely seems as though I had never done, written, spoken, or accomplished anything, when I consider how I am overburdened with things which ought to be written, discussed and treated. But Christ is all and in all, powerful and active, He be blessed in eternity! Amen. . . . You ask me whether I will pray for you. That is what I am doing. Please pray for me too. And just as I don't doubt that your prayers for me can do something, so you shouldn't doubt that mine for you can do something. If I die earlier than you (I hope for that), I will draw you towards me. If you go earlier, draw me with you. For we profess one God and await the Saviour with all the saints.

I have started on a controversial writing—as far as I am able to with God's help—against the theologians of Louvain. For I am more angry with those old fools than is really becoming for a theologian and old man like me. But we have the duty to defy the satanic monsters, even if we had to use up our last breath against them. Farewell! And know that you are my dearest friend, not only because of our true, old friendship, but also for Christ's sake, whom we with the same doctrine profess together. We are sinners, but He is our righteousness, who lives for ever and ever. Amen.[5]

"Against the asses from Paris and Louvain" the book would be called. On the 23rd of January 1546, he took leave of his wife for the last time to travel to Eisleben with his three sons (Hans, Martin and Paul), his assistant Johan Aurifaber, and some servants. He had the manuscript in his suitcase. On the way he worked at it, but got only as far as the introduction. It would have been his two hundred eighth publication.

---

[5]WA, Br., xi, 263 f. (17-7-1546).

That Sunday was spent at Halle with the superintendent Justus Jonas. Luther preached in the parish church. During the meal he presented Jonas with an ornamental goblet on which the following words had been engraved:

To Jonas, who is like a glass, Luther, also like a glass, gives this glass, that both of them may remember: we are all like fragile glass.

Jonas joined the travellers. But on Monday morning it proved to be impossible to continue the journey. The river Saale was flooded and the ferrymen considered the crossing dangerous. In a humorous letter Luther writes about the delay to his wife:

"Grace and peace from the Lord be with you. Dear Katie, this morning at eight o'clock we left Halle but we have not journeyed on to Eisleben. At nine o'clock we entered Halle again. We met with a great lady of the Anabaptist persuasion, covering the land with high waves and big ice-floes and threatening to baptize us. Neither can we go back, because of the river Mulde, and thus we are caught here at Halle between the waters. We do not, however, quench our thirst with them! We take good Torgau beer for that and good Rhenish wine, and with this we refresh and comfort ourselves in the meantime. We do hope that the Saale will rage itself out today. The ferrymen and the postillons did not want to risk the crossing and so we did not dare to go on the water either; it would have been tempting God. For the devil is down on us and he lives in the waters. Therefore we had better be careful and not give the Pope and his company any reason for frantic joy. I never realized that the Saale could have formed such a mass of waters and could have flooded everything so widely. But this will do for to-day. Pray for us and bear up bravely. I think that if you had been here, you would have given the same advice to us. So you see that we do follow up your advice after all. God be with you! Amen. On the day of the conversion of St. Paul, when we converted from the Saale in the direction of Halle. 1546."[6]

It was Thursday before they could leave. An escort of honor consisting of 130 horsemen waited for the reformer at the boundary of the county of Mansfeld. On the way Luther stepped out and went on foot for a while to get some exercise. Owing to the bleak wind he seems to have caught a cold and he was taken with a fit of dizziness. "Now, those are always the devil's tricks," he said. "When I start on some important business he tries to make it impossible for me with his attacks." But at night, in the house of the municipal secretary Joh. Albrecht, he felt all right. Albrecht was a good friend of his. He had invited Luther to stay with him and had offered his house as a place for the discussions with the counts and their lawyers.

Legal, dynastic, financial, economic and social issues were demanding a solution. That is to say: matters of the secular realm. One could justly ask what Luther as a theologian had to do with it. Indeed, he was the man who again and again had warned people not to confuse matters of spiritual and secular areas. He considered it one of the most important results of the reformation—and he was certainly right in this—that the dominance of the church in secular matters, which was usual in the Middle Ages, had come to an end. He was proud of it. In 1520 he had thrown the canon law together with the papal bull of excommunication into the fire. Pope and emperor, church and state, the Gospel and politics ought to keep within their own bounds and should not be allowed to encroach one upon another.

And what is he himself doing now? He, a doctor of theology, reformer, is going to make decisions in matters

---

[6]WA, Br., xi, 269 (25-1-1546).

which essentially belong to the secular sphere. However, one thing is obvious: he did not do so as a theologian, as a teacher of the church or a minister of religion. He did it as a human being and a Christian. For in his doctrine of the two kingdoms he had said just this, time and again: Every Christian has the duty, with the means given to him by *ratio* (reason) and love, to take an active part in social and political life wherever he is called upon. Luther did not speak in these last days in Eisleben as a spiritual and ecclesiastical leader but as a son of his native country whose public position permitted him to act with authority as an intermediary.

And in this last problem with which he had to deal it became clear to him once more that judicial and political questions are, in essence, questions of inter-human relations, of the human heart. They can therefore not be solved by the theories of lawyers and politicians, but only by the Christian man called upon by God. Such a man does not collect his wisdom from codes of law, but in the actual relations between living human beings makes his decisions according to his wise insight and sound judgment. Many times he had emphasized this point in his writings. Now he would prove it with his last deed, his last energies.

The negotiations were dragging on with difficulty. Several times during those three weeks Luther was on the point of going back to Wittenberg, as is clear from letters to his wife and Melanchthon.[7] Most of all he often despaired of the lawyers whom he had never liked very much. But he persevered out of love for his country, as he writes, realizing that the counts would at last be willing to settle the dispute for his sake.

---

[7]WA, Br., xi, 277, 285, 286 f, 301. (7, 6, 7, 14-2-1546).

During his stay he preached in St. Andreas church four times, and he even consecrated there two clergymen "according to old apostolic rites." At supper he was always cheerful and talkative. His hosts took excellent care of him. The city council provided a good supply of wine every day and the beer in Eisleben was very good in his opinion.[8] Every evening at eight o'clock he retired to his bedroom which was kept especially warm for him and in which his sons and Justus Jonas slept with him. Then he prayed aloud, as was his habit, standing in front of the window. "After that he turned away from the window as if he had laid down a burden, talked to us for a quarter of an hour and went to bed," his friends tell us.

Meanwhile Katharina, who had gone through so many difficulties with him and knew that he would not be able to stand much more, was at home and very anxious. She had misgivings about him and his mission in Eisleben. In his delightful witty letters to her—as many as six have been preserved—Luther makes light of her anxieties: "It's you who want to take care instead of God, as if He were not Almighty. He can make ten new *doctores Martinos* if this old one is drowned in the Saale or is killed in the stove or on the finchery of Wolf [his servant]. Don't annoy me with your anxiety. I have someone who takes better care of me than you and all the angels together. He, who lies in the manger, at the breast of a virgin, but who nevertheless sits on the right hand of God, the almighty Father."[9] A few days later he mockingly thanks her for her great solicitude. Because, thanks to her care, a fire broke out in his room, and the next day a big stone falling from the ceiling

[8] WA, Br., xi, 287 (7-2-1546).
[9] WA, Br., xi, 286 (7-2-1546).

101

almost hit him on his head. "I fear that if you don't stop being fearful for me, the earth will swallow us up and all elements will persecute us. Is that what you have learned in the Catechism and the Creed? Only pray and let God care. No one has charged you to take care of me or of yourself as it is written: 'Cast thy burden upon the Lord and He shall sustain thee,' Psalm 55:22 and many other places."[10]

During the last decades of his life many people often came to Luther asking him to write a dedication in their copies of one of his writings (usually a postil or Bible translation). Most frequently he did so with reference to a word from the Scriptures. Quite soon collections were made of these dedications and so a large number has been preserved to us.[11] Among these there is one which Luther wrote in the postil of one of his acquaintances, a land agent from Honstein who visited him in Eisleben a week before his death. Its starting point is St. John 8:51, a text which he often used on such occasions: "Verily, verily, I say unto you, if a man keep my saying he shall never see death." To this he added: "How incredible is such a word. It is directly against our everyday experiences, and yet it is the truth. If a man earnestly considers God's Word in his heart and in this faith, trusting in Him, falls asleep or dies, then he sinks down and passes away before he is conscious of it and without becoming aware of death. Then he has undoubtedly departed this life blessed in believing this word."[12]

On Sunday the 14th of February Luther wrote his last letter to his wife. It has a cheerful tone. The negotiations are almost finished. He hopes to come back home

[10]WA, Br., xi, 291 (10-2-1546).
[11]WA, xlviii, I-297.
[12]WA, xlviii, 162

this week, God willing. The young people of the family of the count, he relates, ride in horse-drawn sleighs and play winter games. He sends his wife some trout, a present from the countess, who is glad that the dispute in her family has been settled. The boys have gone to Mansfeld where they are well lodged with Luther's brother Jacob. There are rumors of war, he writes at the end of his letter. The emperor seems to be near, the count (of Hessen) is mobilizing. "Let them talk whatever they want. We shall wait for God's will. God be with you! Amen."[13]

The next day, Monday, the 15th of February, he preached his last sermon in St. Andreas church. His text was Matthew 11:25: "These things are hid from the wise and prudent but thou hast revealed them unto babes." His sermon is a bold summary of one of the central thoughts of his theology. He concludes with the words: "Much more is to be said about this word from the Scripture, but I am too infirm and this will do."

During the next days the discussions were closed. In two documents Luther summarized his intermediary statement.[14] The legal philosopher from Berlin, Rudolf Stammler, has stated in several studies,[15] that from the standpoint of critical legal theory Luther's decisions were excellent, and bear evidence of penetrating insight and prudent judgment. Characteristically Luther chalked an aphorism on the wall of his room: "We cannot do what everyone wants us to do—but we can do what we want." The last two evenings at supper there were talks about

---

[13]WA, Br., xi, 300 (14-2-1546).
[14]*Erl. Ausg.*, 17, Nr. 3622, 3624.
[15]Rudolf Stammler, "Luther im Schiedsgericht der Grafen von Mansfeldt," in *Was Luther uns heute noch ist*, 1917, 129-141. Ibid., "Luthers letzte Lebenstat," in *Zeitschr. f. syst. Theol.*, II (1924-25, 595-604. Ibid., *Deutsches Rechtsleben in alter und neuer Zeit*, I, 1928, 105-118.

death and eternity. Luther felt his end approaching. On Tuesday he spoke the well-known words full of that grim, yet pious self-ridicule which is characteristic of him: "When I shall come back to Wittenberg, I shall lie down in the coffin and feed the worms with a sturdy doctor."[16] During the last meal, Wednesday night, the question whether the blessed in heaven will recognize each other was discussed. When his friends urged Luther to give his opinion about this he said:

What happened to Adam? He had never seen Eve in his life. He lay down and slept when it happened. And yet when he woke up he did not say: where do you come from, who are you? But he said: This is now bone of my bone and flesh of my flesh (Gen. 2:23). How did he know that this woman had not sprung from a stone? Because he was full of the Holy Ghost and inspired with the knowledge of God. Presently, in eternal life, we are renewed in Christ to that true knowledge and original image that Adam had in Paradise so that we shall recognize our father and mother and each other face to face better than Adam recognized Eve. [17]

Then came the last night, about which a great number of legendary stories exists. For some time it had been the habit of antagonists to ascribe the birth and death of their opponents to the devil. Consequently, Luther's appearance in this world was ascribed to direct interference by Satan, and his end should have been at least that of a suicide.[18] We possess, however, two reliable eye-witness

[16]WA, T., vi, Nr. 6975 (16-2-1546).

[17]WA, liv, 489 (Jonas and Coelius, Bericht von christlichen Abschied Lutheri).

[18]Cf. Karl Schottenloher, *Bibliographie zur deutschen Geschichte im Zeitalter der Glaubensspaltung,* I, Nr. 12963-13005. See also: Gustav Kawerau, *Luthers Lebensende in neuester ultramontaner Beleuchtung,* 1890[4]. Theodor Kolde, *Luthers Lebensende. Eine Geschichtslüge P. Majunkes beleuchtet,* 1890[5] N. Paulus, *Luthers Lebensende und der Eislebener Apotheker Johann Landau,* 1896. Karl Kampffmeyer und Wolfram Schulze, *Luthers Tod, die Juden und Melanchthon. Die sachlichen*

reports, one from Luther's friend, Justus Jonas, and the other from the Roman Catholic apothecary, Witzel. We are able to reconstruct the course of events in this last night with certainty.[19]

✗ After his evening prayers Luther suffered a heart attack. "I think I will stay here at Eisleben where I was born and baptized," he said to his friend Jonas. The latter has handed down to us the fervent prayer in which the dying man commended himself in God's love: "My heavenly Father, eternal, merciful God. Thou revealed to me Thy beloved Son, our Lord Jesus Christ. Him I did preach, I love and worship Him as my dear Lord and Savior, abused and scolded by the wicked. Take my little soul unto Thee." "In this childlike prayer," Heinrich Bornkamm says, "this life with its striking activity and readiness to fight, but just because of this with its terrible inner temptations and anguish, finally came to rest."[20] Thereupon Luther recited in Latin Psalm 68:19, 20: "Blessed be the Lord, who daily loadeth us with benefits, even the God of our salvation; and unto God the Lord belong the issues from death." And then three times, quickly and one after the other, as prescribed in the *Completorium*, the evening prayers and the medieval prayers for dying men: "*In manus tuas, domine,*

_____

Unterlagen zur Beurteilung der von Frau M. Ludendorff aufgestellten Behauptungen über Luther Lebensende, 1933. In some Roman-Catholic propaganda in tracts and other popular literature in America the old legends about Luther's suicide have unfortunately been revived.

[19]J. Strieder, *Authentische Berichte über Luthers letzte Lebensstunden* (Kleine Texte Lietzmann), 1912. Christof Schubart, *Die Berichte über Luthers Tod und Begräbnis, Texte und Untersuchungen,* 1917. Theodor Knolle, *D. Martin Luthers letzte Tagen im Zeugnis seiner letzten Briefe, Tischreden, Predigten, Schriften und seiner Freunde,* 1946.

[20]Heinrich Bornkamm, *Luthers geistige Welt,* 1953,[2] 343. (English translation by Martin H. Bertram, *Luther's World of Thought.*)

commendo spiritum meum. Lord, into Thy hands I commit my spirit."

Another heart attack struck him. The Count of Mansfeld came with his wife, two doctors and an apothecary. They tried all possible means, but efforts to revive him were of no avail. He could no longer speak. Only once, when one of the friends asked: "Your Reverend Father, you do profess Christ, the Son of God, our Lord and Savior, don't you?" he answered: "Yes." Then he turned on his right side, and with clasped hands he fell asleep quietly. It was between two and three o'clock in the night.

He died just as he had lived. He did not ask for a priest or the extreme unction. He departed after having finished his daily task, as he had sung in his German version of the *Nunc dimittis:* "In peace and joy I now depart."

The two doctors were not yet agreed what sort of apoplexy he had had. But Melanchthon, who had studied medicine briefly and who knew Luther so well, said that he died of cardiogmus, which we call angina pectoris. Melanchthon was probably correct.[21]

The next morning his assistant Johann Aurifaber found in the death-room a small sheet of paper on which Luther, shortly before his death, had written down his spiritual will in abrupt clauses. He made a copy of it at once. Justus Jonas kept the original. The notes were in Latin:

1. Vergil's *Bucolica* and *Georgica* [his pastoral and rustic poems] cannot be understood by anyone unless he has been a shepherd or farmer for five years.

---

[21]Paul J. Reiter, *Martin Luthers Umwelt, Charakter und Psychose.*, II. *Luthers Persönlichkeit, Seelenleben und Krankheiten*, 1941. Karl Müller, "Noch ein Wort zu Luthers letzte Krankheit und Tod," in *Zeitschr. f. Kirchengesch.*, 46 (1928), 407-409.

2. Cicero in his letters (I dare say) cannot be understood by anyone unless he has been versed in "high level" politics for twenty-five years.

3. Nobody should think he has enjoyed enough Holy Scripture if he has not guided the Church with the prophets for a hundred years. And so the miracle of John the Baptist, of Christ and the apostles is very great indeed. Do not try to follow this divine Aeneid journey, but kneel down in worship with bowed heads over the imprints where He has stepped.[22] We are beggars *(Wir sind Bettler)*. That is true *(Hoc est verum)*.[23]

Here the experience of a whole lifetime is summarized: nature which he loved; the world which fascinated him; God's Word which meant everything to him. With great reverence Luther approaches the mystery of the three spheres of life. No writing, he says, is to be understood from the outside; only from the inside may it be opened by him who is spiritually akin to the writer. If the life of the countryman has its secrets, greater are those of the statesman. Anyone who wants to become familiar with their writings will have to spend from five to twenty-five years to enter into the spirit of and sympathize with that particular world.

Marvellous however is the secret of the Bible. All his life Luther had been absorbed in it. And now at the end of it, he says: it is beyond all comprehension. This is not a matter of theoretical knowledge, of studying or learning. One becomes at home in God's Word only if one lives in it, amidst the Church, with John, with Christ,

---

[22]The Aeneid tells of the wanderings and struggles of the Trojan Aeneas which finally led to the foundation of the Roman empire and of the city of Rome. Luther compares the Bible, or rather the history of grace contained in it, to the Aeneid because the Bible tells us of the difficulties God has with His people in order to found the Church of the New Testament and the city of God. This sentence is a distichon from Statius, *Thebais*, XII, 816 f.

[23]WA, T., v, Nr. 5677

with the apostles. Do not try to follow God's way through the world but kneel down in worship with bowed heads over His holy footprints, given to us in the Scriptures. A hundred years one needs for it. That is to say: no one will ever have completed it. For who gets older than a hundred years? In Luther's days certainly nobody. Our life is too short to fully comprehend the Bible. The man who for scores of years had engrossed himself in the secrets of God's Word warns us just before his death: we are beggars, that is true.

And because he was a beggar who lived in God's plentiful mercy the following word from the Psalms holds good for him. It was a word which he loved above all, and which he wrote down together with the music on the wall of his room during one of the most difficult periods of his life: "I shall not die, but live, and declare the works of the Lord" (Psalm 118:17).

Lowell C. Green

Luther and
Melanchthon

The Young and the Mature Luther

Melanchthon in His Relation to Luther

The Renaissance in Lutheran Theology

The Young and the Mature Luther

ONE of the more dramatic stories connected with modern research in Luther has to do with the discovery of the Lectures on Romans. For years it had been known that Luther had lectured on Romans, though no one knew just when, and no copy of the lectures had been found. It must have seemed a great misfortune to Protestant historians when the Catholic writer on Luther, Heinrich Denifle, began to quote from Luther's lectures on Romans, and used them in the attempt to discredit the reformer.

How was Denifle able to do this? A student's copybook containing the long-lost lectures had turned up in the Vatican library, and was at first restricted to Roman Catholic scholars. So fine a scholar as Friedrich Loofs was obliged to draw certain of his Luther citations from Denifle's treatise in the attempt to refute the latter. Meanwhile scholars continued their search for other copies. It was an irony of history that, when Luther's own personal copy of the lectures was found, it was discovered in a glass showcase in the lobby of the Royal

Library of Berlin, where thousands of people had passed it year after year, unheedingly. To Johannes Ficker goes the honor of discovering that the stately volume, which was bound in a luxurious leather cover, decorated with the coat-of-arms and initials of the Elector August of Saxony, and bearing the misleadingly late date of 1582, actually contained the long-lost autograph of Luther's Lectures on Romans as he delivered them in 1515 and 1516.

The publication in 1908 of the Lectures on Romans proved to be a great stimulus to Luther research. Out of these Lectures, taken together with other early works of Luther, there emerged a new portrait of the reformer. Scholars began to speak of the "young Luther." They pointed out that much of the earlier study in Luther's career had produced a one-sided picture of the man, since it had leaned heavily on his later writings. With improved techniques in historical research utilized, the early writings of Luther were subjected to an investigation of unprecedented intensiveness. It soon became fashionable to play the younger Luther against the older man. The result was that the new understanding of Luther came to be even more one-sided than the older view. The more mature works of Luther were left in comparative neglect. The task of applying the same careful historical methods to the works of the "mature Luther" lies before us.

It is therefore most praiseworthy that our sponsoring college should devote the 1958 Luther Lectures to the study of the later years of Luther. In many ways the young Luther is more interesting than the older man. He yields forceful paradoxes and pithy quotations that seem to outshine those of the mature Luther. But it is important to remember that the younger Luther cannot safely be cited as representing the final position of Luther the reformer. He was in the process of becoming that mighty instrument in God's hand through which the Gospel was restored to the Church. Whereas the earliest works of Luther often produce statements in which Luther is still a son of Rome, his later works show a comprehensiveness and maturity often absent from the writings of his formative period.

Such considerations make it clear that Luther research today cannot content itself with studying the works of only a certain period, for this can yield only a partial Luther. What is needed, if we are to speak of Luther's position with some measure of confidence, is a study embracing the various stages of Luther's development. Such breadth is certainly necessary, e.g., for an understanding of his political ethics, or of his teaching on the Lord's Supper. For the present, however, we are especially interested in his doctrine of justification. A study of Luther's teaching concerning justification will reveal that it is impossible to understand what he taught unless we see it against the background of a process of gradual personal development.

1. *Luther's development from 1512 to 1519*

One often hears the opinion expressed in the United States that so much study has been devoted to Luther that little remains to be done. I must disagree. Rather, each stride forward in our understanding of this great man reveals new areas where we are in ignorance. Luther's first seven years as professor at Wittenberg constitute what is perhaps the most baffling period of his life. The so-called tower experience has never been satisfactorily explained.

As recently as 1923, the great Luther scholar Johannes

von Walter admitted that the true significance of the tower experience was still unknown. Friedrich Loofs wrote some years earlier that no scholar, whether Julius Köstlin, Otto Scheel, Karl Holl, or Loofs himself, had ever reached satisfactory conclusions as to the meaning of *iustitia Dei*, the righteousness of God, a term intimately connected with Luther's doctrine of justification and the problem of the tower experience.[1] Since the days of these giants in Luther research, considerable advance has been made in solving these problems. The Finnish-American theologian, Uuras Saarnivaara, gives us the best summary in English of previous research, and an original solution of his own that is very plausible.[2] Saarnivaara correctly notes that Luther did not come to a full understanding of the righteousness of God before 1519, and concludes that the tower experience should be dated at the end of 1518. We may support Saarnivaara in noting Luther's change at the end of 1518, but to date the initial experience of justification so late appears to be untenable. It is unthinkable that the great works of the young Luther, such as his brilliant commentaries on Romans, Galatians, and Hebrews, his exposition of the Seven Penitential Psalms, or the Ninety-Five Theses, should have been produced before Luther's first awakening to the meaning of the Evangel.

Shall we attempt to solve the riddle differently? Let us seek to establish two different experiences of Luther: first, a religious awakening that was identical with the tower experience, dated as early as 1513 or 1514; and

---

[1] Johannes von Walter, "Der Abschluss der Entwickelung des jungen Luther," in *Zeitschrift für systematische Theologie* (1923), I, 412 ff. Friedrich Loofs, " 'Iustitia dei passiva' in Luthers Anfängen," in *Theologische Studien und Kritiken*, (1911), v. 84, 466-467.

[2] Uuras Saarnivaara, *Luther Discovers the Gospel*. St. Louis, 1951, 48, 92 ff.

second, a theological discovery, dated in 1518 or 1519. Then we shall attempt to show that only such a hypothesis can bring together the seemingly contradictory evidence.

No one has explained the tower experience with greater plausibility than Erich Vogelsang, who dated it 1513-1514. Vogelsang was a rare combination of literary critic and theologian. Working on the basis of the autographical text of Luther's first Lectures on the Psalms, Vogelsang, with an unusual empathy, takes his reader into Luther's study as the young monk, preparing his lectures, was fearfully confronted by the God of righteousness whom he was so desperately trying to understand. Vogelsang shows that this conflict reached a preliminary crisis as Luther, working on Psalm 31, was unable to solve the riddle, but had at any rate been faced with it. During his lectures on Psalm 70, Luther was still in the dark, except that he was beginning to relate the righteousness of God to the doctrine of Christ. But suddenly, while Luther was preparing his lectures on Psalm 71, the evangelical truth dawned upon him. For the first time he began to understand Romans 1:17: "For therein is the righteousness of God revealed from faith to faith, as it is written, 'The just shall live by faith.'" Luther then explained that troublesome phrase, the righteousness of God, as follows: ". . . Righteousness, namely that by which He makes us brave, in which He saves us, in which He *makes us righteous*. . . ."[3] This point, according to Vogelsang, marks the beginning of Luther's radical understanding of justification.

In accepting Vogelsang's analysis, however, we should

---

[3]The reference to Psalm 71 is found in WA iii, 461 ff. The page references in the text above are to Erich Vogelsang, *Die Anfänge von Luthers Christologie, nach der ersten Psalmenvorlesung* . . . Berlin, 1929. See especially pages 40 ff, 48 f.

beware of the popular opinion of the tower experience as the moment of discovering the Gospel in its fullest sense. The truth is that Luther still stood a long way from his mature doctrine of justification. Some historians, taking it for granted that Luther had reached his full understanding of justification so early, have allowed this misconception to affect their findings in studying the young Luther. Hence they often read into his early writings doctrines which were simply not yet developed.

It might be salutary to review, however sketchily, Luther's limitations in this early period. Even when Luther posted the Ninety-Five Theses on October 31, 1517, he still was far removed from his later theology.[4] He was as yet more "Catholic" than "Lutheran." In 1517 Luther was still an Augustinian monk occupying a prominent position and enjoying good standing in his order. He taught the existence of purgatory and continued to hold masses as a Roman Catholic priest. He accepted the authority of the pope. He had not yet found his way to saying that the Holy Scriptures could be held up against the authority of Rome. In 1517 Luther still accepted the medieval teaching of transubstantiation in regard to the Lord's Supper. He still venerated the Blessed Virgin Mary and the saints. Nor had he succeeded in throwing off the medieval doctrine of faith. When Luther launched his attack on the indulgence traffic, he did not intend to abolish indulgences themselves, but was merely trying to make an end to the abuses which had come to pervade the churchly practices.

---

[4]Bainton's statement in this connection could be misunderstood when he writes: "Luther's new insights contained already the marrow of his mature theology. The salient ideas were present in the lectures on Psalms and Romans from 1513 to 1516. What came after was but commentary and sharpening to obviate misconstruction." Roland Bainton, *Here I Stand*. New York, 1950, 68.

When Luther nailed the Ninety-Five Theses to the door of the Castle Church at Wittenberg, he still had two great hurdles over which he later had to leap. He had to discover the evangelical doctrine of justification, and following this, to throw off the yoke of Roman authoritarianism. Both of these fundamental reformational insights first appeared in 1519.

If all of this seems too negative, then hear Luther's own statement about his development during 1512 to 1519, as we find it in the Preface to his Latin works of 1545:

> Publicly and privately, I have read and taught the Holy Scriptures for seven years with great diligence, so that I knew almost all of them by memory. In that time I had gained my first knowledge of Christ and faith in Him, namely, that Christ makes us righteous and saves us, not by works but by faith. . . .[5]

But now Luther went on to show that this *primitias cognitionis et fidei*, this "first knowledge of Christ and faith in Him," was only the start. He did not know the evangelical doctrine of justification before 1519. According to his own statement, he first learned to understand the phrase *iustitia Dei passiva*, or justifying righteousness of God, in the year 1519.[6] As a matter of fact, this phrase is scarcely to be found in the early writings of Luther.

When Luther in 1545 made public this reminiscence of his development, he applied a term which he had actually developed later than 1519. Nevertheless the discovery of the passive righteousness of God can be traced back to that year. There are earlier instances in Luther where it may appear that he is speaking of passive right-

---

[5]WA liv, 183.
[6]WA lvi, 185.

eousness.[7] But the term itself does not occur, and he is speaking of something else. In 1519 we find the first real occurrence of the concept, though the phrase itself does not yet appear. In the tower experience Luther first realized that the righteousness of God referred to in Romans 1:17 was not that attribute in which God was righteous in Himself, but rather the righteousness with which He clothed man when He justified the sinner. Nevertheless these words were not original. They were a quotation from Augustine's work *De Spiritu et Litera.*[8] Before 1519 Luther had not gone much beyond Augustine in his understanding of the righteousness of God.

After the tower experience, and during the first stage of his development, Luther understood passive righteousness as something that was developed by God within man, that is, as *analytic* righteousness. Hence Luther could offer the following comment on Romans 4:7: "Thus our righteousness from God is the same inclination to good and abhorrence of evil as it is given us inwardly through grace."[9] This early doctrine of righteousness must be studied against the background of Luther's distinction between *opera legis* and *fidei,* that is, works of the Law and works of faith. Luther rejected all works that man might try to bring forth of himself to fulfill the Law, for he saw that such works had no worth in the sight of God, polluted as they are by spiritual pride and prompted by the desire to further one's

---

[7] Here a word of warning is in order against confusing the terms *justificatio passiva* and *iustitia passiva.* Both Friedrich Loofs *(Op. cit.)* and Erich Seeberg make this mistake. Erich Seeberg, *Luthers Theologie in ihren Grundzügen.* Stuttgart, 1950, 19.

[8] This Luther acknowledged in his Preface of 1545, WA liv, 186. His indebtedness to Augustine was also acknowledged in the *Scholia* to Rom. 1:17, WA lvi. The reference from Augustine is found in Book IX, 15 of his *De Spiritu et Litera,* CSEL VIII/I, 657.

[9] WA lvi, 271.

118

own ends. But works of faith, *opera fidei*, played a role in his early teaching on justification. These were good works developed by God Himself to provide a basis for an analytic justification.[10] Their performance was made possible through faith in Christ. In his Lectures on Galatians of 1516-1517, Luther offered this explanation of Galatians 2:16:

> Therefore salvation and righteousness can neither be had without works nor from works, but only with works. Yet it is with this difference: as soon as they increase inwardly and become perfect, the outward works diminish that much more.[11]

It is against this background that we ought to consider Karl Holl's construction of Luther's doctrine of justification. Soon after Johannes Ficker had published the first edition of the Lectures on Romans, Karl Holl wrote an essay which evoked a controversy which has remained alive. Holl proceeded on the basis of Luther's exegesis of Romans 4:7: "Blessed are they whose iniquities are forgiven, and whose sins are covered." Here is the crucial question: Was Luther speaking of an intrinsic righteousness within the believer (the "analytic" view), or did he have in mind the righteousness of Christ imputed to the believer by grace (the "synthetic" view)?

---

[10]This distinction seems to have been a forerunner of the distinction between Law and Gospel as it later developed. The earlier form had these earmarks: 1) *Opera legis* remained under the Law's compulsion, while *opera fidei* were freely done through faith. 2) *Opera legis* sprang from self-love and the desire to be saved, whereas *opera fidei* were done out of a pure love for God, which went so far as the *resignatio ad infernum*. 3) *Opera legis* tried to satisfy the Law, while *opera fidei* tried to please only God. 4) *Opera legis* drew pride from a righteousness which they imagined they already possessed, but *opera fidei* were characterized by humility and the desire for perfected righteousness still to come. See *Schol.* to Rom. 3:20, WA lvi 2 54 f.; *Schol.* to Rom. 3:28, WA lvi, 264; *Schol.* to Gal. 2:3, WA lvii/2, 63, 68.

[11]WA lvii/2, 68.

Listen to Luther's interpretation of Romans 4:7, as he employs the parable of the Good Samaritan to give his views in 1515:

> In the same way, Christ, our Good Samaritan, took the sick man, half dead, to the inn, in order to cure him. And He began to heal him with the promise of perfected healing in eternal life, not imputing his sin . . . unto death. But in the meantime, offering him the hope of promised healing, He commanded him to do and leave undone those things which interfered with the recovery, or by which sin . . . might be increased. Has the man therefore become perfectly righteous? No. He is at once a sinner and a righteous man. He is a sinner in actuality, but he is righteous on the basis of how God regards him and what God promises to make of him, absolving him from sin until he is perfectly healed. And so the man is healed perfectly in hope, but in actuality he is still a sinner. He has the beginning of righteousness, the more he realizes that he is unrighteous.[12]

If we analyze this statement, we see that justification is here regarded as a healing process that takes place within the man rather than a forensic act. This teaching is not far removed from Augustine's theology. When Holl said that Luther taught an analytic justification in this passage, we can only agree with him. Holl adds: "Just as a great artist envisions beforehand his finished statue in the raw block of marble, so God sees in advance the righteous man that He shall form, in the sinner that He declares just."[13] Holl is right when he gives his presentation of Luther's doctrine of justification, so long as he confines it to the young Luther. But when he goes on to say that Luther never rose above this pre-reformational view, he no longer has the facts in his support.

Now let us return to Luther's Preface of 1545. In look-

---

[12]WA lvi, 272.

[13]Karl Holl, *Gesammelte Aufsätze zur Kirchengeschichte.* 7. aufl. Tübingen, 1948, I, 125

ing back over his development from 1512 to 1519, the mature Luther confessed that he had got no farther than to the "first knowledge of Christ and faith in Him." We are not surprised at this judgment, since we have examined his earlier teaching and found it to be pre-reformational. We find no need to refute his words of 1545, as so many have attempted to do, since Luther tells us that in 1519, when he had begun to lecture on the Book of Psalms for the second time, he had still not solved the problem of the interpretation of those fateful words, the righteousness of God.[14] Day and night Luther sought to understand Romans 1:17. Finally the truth dawned on him that God saves the believing sinner through a passive righteousness, *iustitia passiva*.[15]

It may appear, at this point, as though I were trying to discourage a study of the young Luther. That has not been my intention. The writings and lectures from the dawn of the Reformation are fascinating reading, and are surely necessary for an understanding of Martin Luther. But it is necessary that when we study them we do so with an understanding of the historical problems involved. If we are unaware of them, we shall be susceptible to one of two errors. Either we shall not get a true picture of the young Luther, or else we shall not be able to come to terms with his teachings in the period of his maturity. If however there are important differences between the various periods of Luther, ought we not be able to find passages in the mature Luther in which he comments on the theology of his earlier

[14]WA liv, 185.

[15]Luther says that he came to realize that *iustitia* referred not to the righteousness with which God Himself was righteous, but that with which He endowed the believer in justification. Part of this Luther had learned earlier in the tower experience, but its full implications did not occur to him until his further progress in 1519. WA liv, 186.

years? Actually such passages are not at all difficult to find.

2. The Mature Luther's Evaluation of His Earlier Theology

We have already examined Luther's observation made in 1545 that his theology from 1512 until 1519 represented only "the first knowledge of Christ and faith in Him." In the same Preface he gives a more negative criticism of the young Luther. He writes:

> So in my former writings you can find many important places where I basely made concessions to the pope. These earlier statements I now hold to be the height of blasphemy and do solemnly condemn them as an abomination.[16]

Luther could hardly have spoken more vigorously, for he here repudiated his pre-reformational theology in language as unsparing as that which he usually applied only to enemies of the Gospel. But this is not an isolated statement. In 1528 Luther wrote his testament in which he made it abundantly clear that he did not want his earlier works to be regarded as authoritative in his theology. In his "Great Confession on the Holy Supper of Christ" he offered a summary of his more mature insights, and then added that readers who wanted to know what he stood for should read his books, "especially those which have gone out more recently in the last four or five years."[17]

If we take this statement literally, we must conclude that in 1528 he no longer recognized the adequacy of books that he had written before 1523. Or are we too much enslaved to the calendar in drawing such a conclusion? For example, can we not accept the so-called

---

[16]WA liv, 179 f.
[17]WA xxvi, 509.

"Short Commentary on Galatians" from 1519 as representing the mature reformer? Yet in 1531 when Luther began his second great series of Lectures on Galatians, he said he was doing so because the earlier work was no longer acceptable. At that time he exclaimed in the *Table Talk:* "I had not realized how weak my first commentaries on Galatians were. Oh, they are worthless for this generation! They were nothing more than my first light against confidence in works."[18] Or could Luther perhaps have meant that the earlier work was too short? The commentary of 1519 comprises only 175 pages in the Weimar Edition of Luther's *Works;* nevertheless in 1523 he had sharply pruned the work down when he prepared a second edition. The new work that he began in 1531 occupies (with its double text) well over 800 pages in two volumes of the Weimar Edition. We cannot easily escape the impression that Luther in 1531 meant to say that he could no longer endorse the content of his commentary of 1519.

3. *Melanchthon's Part in the Development of Luther*

As I introduce this sub-theme, I think no one will accuse me of walking over well-trodden ground. Very little attention has been given to the possibility that Melanchthon might have actually given vital assistance to Luther during the years that he developed his mature theology. Yet Luther would have been far different without both the positive and negative elements of influence from the brilliant young humanist who in 1518 came to Wittenberg to teach Greek grammar and remained to become the father of the German educational system. He became also the first systematic theologian

[18]WA TR. 2, p. 281, No. 1963.

in Lutheranism, as well as the co-worker upon whom Luther most leaned for help.

An interesting indication of how much Luther learned from Melanchthon may be found in the history of Luther's Commentary on Galatians of 1519. Basing it on his Lectures on Galatians of 1516-1517, Luther prepared it for publication in 1518, the year that Master Philip came to teach at Wittenberg.[19] Luther suddenly decided that it was not ready for publication. What had transpired in the meantime? Luther had progressed in two important respects. On the one hand, as already noted, he had discovered new light on the doctrine of the righteousness of God. On the other hand, it was at this time that he finally arrived at his reformational view of faith. Melanchthon had entered the theological as well as the academic scene.

In the revised edition of 1519 Luther offers a new concept of faith, and says explicitly that it was the new Greek teacher at Wittenberg who helped him to arrive at this new understanding. Previously Luther had faltered in the attempt to overcome the medieval doctrine of faith. The scholastic teachers of the Middle Ages had spoken of *fides implicita*, referring to a faith which did not know the Catholic doctrines but accepted them on the authority of the Church, and *fides explicita*, a faith which rested upon an informed knowledge of churchly teachings. But in either case, faith was little more than intellectual assent. Faith was regarded as a *habitus* or condition which was bestowed by God like a substance.[20]

---

[19]Fortunately we possess a copy of the original lectures, as written down by a student in Luther's class, in WA lvii/2, but Luther's own manuscript has never been discovered.

[20]This view, reflected in the *Vulgate*, was preserved in the English Authorized Version: "Faith is the substance of things hoped for . . .," Hebr. 11:1.

Thus faith had nothing to do with *fiducia,* or trust in God. *Fiducia* had been bound scholastically to *spes,* or hope, so that it was related to the future and divorced from the present. Half a year before he met Melanchthon, Luther had wrestled with this problem alone. In lecturing on Hebrews 11:1 he had expressed his dissatisfaction with the view that had come down through the Middle Ages, but he had not been able to solve the problem.[21] It was Melanchthon who helped him to crack this hard shell, in order to uncover the sweet kernel of faith. Under Melanchthon's tutelage, Luther dropped the medieval idea of faith as a *habitus* or infused substance, and correctly defined faith as *fiducia* or trust in God. Luther relates in his own words how he learned this.

Jerome understood faith as described by the apostle in Heb. xi as the "substance of things hoped for" . . . I was also of this opinion for a long time, because I had observed that *substantia* was commonly employed in various parts of the Holy Scriptures to denote capabilities and possession. I held tenaciously to the authority of Jerome on this doctrine. For who would dare to change what the writers of the sentences, in writing on faith, had put within the term *substantia?* But more recently I have followed Philip Melanchthon as my teacher in Greek. He is a young man in respect to his body, but a hoary-headed old sage in regard to his intellectual powers. Melanchthon would not let me understand it thus, and showed me that *substantia,* whenever it signifies a capability, is rendered in Greek, not with *hypostasis* (which word the apostle uses in Heb. xi), but either *ousia, broton,* or *hyparxis.* Then I changed my mind and gave up my opinion that *hypostasis* meant the same as *substantia,* but rather *subsistentia.* . . .[22]

We might add that this word *subsistentia* refers to an existential state of being or attitude, such as one of trust

---

[21]See Luther's exposition of Hebr. 11:1 in WA lvii/1, 226-229.
[22]WA ii, 595.

in God. Thus Melanchthon, the Greek teacher, made an important contribution to Luther's development.[23]

This was what Melanchthon, the Greek teacher, taught Luther. Are we to say then that he was *only* a Greek teacher, or did he also possess gifts as a theologian? Was this insight into the true meaning of faith merely a grammatical observation, or did there lie behind it other deep theological insights of the young Master Philip? If we investigate the sources, we shall discover that Melanchthon's first years at Wittenberg were marked by other such "grammatical" discoveries. For example, (Melanchthon rejected the idea of grace as a substance, just as he had refused to consider faith a substance.) In the medieval view, grace was infused into the faithful as a modern "miracle drug" is injected today. Turning his back permanently on this concept, Melanchthon held that grace meant *favor Dei* or divine mercy.[24]

---

[23]Melanchthon developed this insight in his essay, "Quae sit sententia descriptionis fidei in Epist. ad Hebraeos?" of 1533, CR 10, 696-698. Some common misconstructions of Melanchthon's teaching on faith are refuted here, especially the charge that he defined faith as mere intellectual assent, an assertion often made in recent literature. Against this Melanchthon: "We therefore maintain that this is a true and convenient definition of faith. For faith, concerning which we have here made mention, comprises two parts, knowledge or assent, and trust or an action of the heart. . . .

"Going on, faith is not mere knowledge, but it is further a looking out for the divine promises, that is, trust, by which we hold steadfastly to the promises of God. . . .

"Some recent writers . . . have understood the word faith badly, namely as a word having to do with knowledge such as even the devils have, among whom there is certainly no hope of things not seen."

[24]The earliest instance seems to be in Melanchthon's lectures on Romans of 1519, where he defines: "gratia, hoc est fauor dei." From *Annotationes Philip Melanchthon in Epistolas Pauli Ad Rhomanos Et Corinthios*. Nürnberg, 1522, Fol. Vii. Luther's first use of *gratia* as *favor Dei* appears in the Galatians Commentary of 1519, but he went back later at times to the concept of grace as a substance. Melanchthon did not revert back to the medieval view again.

Furthermore, Melanchthon led the way in developing the forensic character of justification as it has become a central teaching in the Lutheran Church. Was it merely coincidental that it was some months after Melanchthon's arrival at Wittenberg, that is in 1519, that Luther solved the problem of the righteousness of God? We shall not attempt to answer that question now. But we can establish the fact that Melanchthon, beginning in 1519, pioneered in the study of two aspects of the problem as they have come down to our day. The first of these is the doctrine of imputation. Said Melanchthon three times in 1519: *"Omnis iustitia nostra est gratuita dei imputatio,"* that is, all our righteousness is due to the free imputation of God. More clearly than in Luther's writings of the same year, Melanchthon discounted every analytic righteousness, and showed that justifying righteousness is the gift of God.[25]

A popular vulgarization of this teaching, in which imputation becomes unreal, conceives of it in a way not far removed from the medieval doctrine of the storehouse of good works, in which superfluous good works of the saints are transferred to the debit-account of needy sinners. The difference is that the merits of Christ take the place of the supererogatory works of the saints. Such a view is a sad caricature of what Melanchthon taught, or of the intention of the Lutheran Symbols as they developed the doctrine of imputation. What they really said was that by faith the believer apprehends Christ,

---

[25]At some future time I hope to publish some of the evidence for this assertion. The indisputable source is found in the Baccalaureate Theses of September 1519, as quoted above, taken from the new *Studienausgabe* (Bertelsmann, 1951 ff.), 24. Another source is found in the glosses or marginal notations on Romans in Melanchthon's own hand as found in *Christaneum Codex, MS. Nr. 16, Aa 3/4* (Gymnasium Library of the Christaneum at Hamburg-Altona), and a statement in the aforementioned Melanchthon *Annotationes,* Fol. Bi.

who comes to dwell in his heart, thereby bringing him into a new relationship to God. At the same time that faith apprehends Christ, it also receives with Christ His righteousness. When God sees the believing sinner, who has become a dwelling place for His Son, He declares for the sake of Christ and through the work of Christ that that person is righteous in His sight—that is, He justifies him. Thus faith justifies because, and only because, Christ is the subject of that faith. Christ's righteousness is imputed because Christ really dwells in that believing heart.

The other phase of Melanchthon's contribution to forensic righteousness was the insight that just as man is sentenced for his sin before God the Judge, so this condemnation is forensically removed in justification (*coram Deo!*). That means that man in every area of his life is liable before God, and that justification is the declaration of God that the believer's guilt has been absolved before God by Christ's atonement.[26]

Some eminent writers on Luther, notably Karl Holl, have maintained that Luther never accepted or taught the forensic doctrine of justification. Such a statement however cannot be made without ignoring a vast amount of literature from Luther's later years. It was especially in his later lectures on Galatians, Psalms, and Genesis that Luther more and more emphasized the teaching of imputation and the forensic character of justification. While there was a difference in emphasis in the teaching of Melanchthon and the mature Luther, their doctrine of justification was nevertheless basically the same.

Thus far we have covered a lot of ground in our dis-

---

[26]The significance of the forensic nature of justification is discussed by Werner Elert in his essay, "Humanität und Kirche: Zum 450. Geburtstag Melanchthons," in *Zwischen Gnade und Ungnade,* . . . München, 1948, 98 ff.

cussion of the young and the mature Luther. We have
been absorbed by the fascinating drama in which the
young monk of the Augustinian monastery at Wittenberg struggles to free himself from the grip of medieval
theology and philosophy as they had obscured the Gospel. We have discovered that this young man could produce exciting theological works. Yet in his later years,
the more mature man said that, whatever their value,
these earlier works should not be regarded as presenting
his reformational theology, but that he saw in his career
a gradual development in his grasp of evangelical truth.
And Philip Melanchthon had played an important part
in Luther's theological development.

4. The Young and the Mature Luther
in Subsequent History

Did the earlier analytic justification taught by the
young Luther now die out completely, or did it live on
in the history of Lutheranism? It lived on for a few
years in one of the surprising episodes of the story of
the Evangelical Lutheran Church. It proved to be the
irony in the life of Andreas Osiander that he was drawn
into the reforming movement in the early 1520's when
Luther's earlier doctrine of justification had not yet been
superseded. In 1522 Osiander became the pastor of the
great Gothic St. Lorenz Church of Nürnberg, where in
the same year he introduced the Lutheran reformation.
In subsequent years he was of decisive importance in
the introduction of the reformation to Nürnberg and
many other parts of Germany. Osiander, one of the most
brilliant men of his time, associated with the circles of
the humanists. It was Osiander who helped sponsor the
first edition of Copernicus' epoch-making work *De revolu-
tionibus orbium coelestium* when it appeared in 1543.

129

Osiander was an independent kind of man. For some time it had been clear that he had not personally accepted the forensic view of justification as it had been developing at Wittenberg. But it was not until after Luther's death that the great controversy over justification broke out between Osiander and Melanchthon. Osiander held that justification took place on the basis of inner renewal that resulted from the indwelling of Christ. In opposition Melanchthon reaffirmed the forensic doctrine of justification. Here again it was a form of the medieval, analytic doctrine of justification that Osiander was unconsciously holding out against the view which had already obtained confessional sanction in the young Lutheran Church. Osiander was fighting a losing battle. The controversy that had been aroused continued until a peaceful solution was reached in the Formula of Concord. At this time the following statement was issued against any analytic type of justification:

> We believe, teach, and confess that our righteousness before God is this very thing, that God forgives our sins out of pure grace, without any respect to our own work, merit, or worthiness, whether preceding, accompanying, or following. God gives and imputes to us the righteousness of Christ's obedience, for whose righteousness' sake we are received by God in grace and regarded as just.[27]

During the age of Lutheran Orthodoxy this issue was no longer a problem. Luther's early Lectures on Romans and other works in which the analytic view had been presented had been largely forgotten. Then during the age of Rationalism, the doctrine of justification as taught by the mature Luther and as written in the Lutheran Confessions became the object of great displeasure. The great Luther Renaissance which began three quarters

---

[27] Lutheran church. *Formula of Concord.* Epitome, Article III, par. 2.

of a century ago rediscovered the young Luther. Since
they came out of the liberal tradition, it was only to be
expected that many of these great Luther scholars should
have been overjoyed to discover Luther's earlier doctrine
of justification. Even today there are loud voices dis-
claiming forensic justification, labelling it as "legalistic,"
and calling us to return to the theology of the young
Luther. Nevertheless this is deceiving. The analytic justification does not offer the freedom and peace that it
seemingly bestows, but leads back to bondage to the
Law as Luther knew it before his final emancipation in
1519. (It is the forensic view alone which declares that
the reign of the Law is ended, and that God, without
any merit or worthiness on our part, but solely for the
sake of Christ, is pleased to regard us as righteous, and
to declare us pardoned from all our guilt and free from
the accusations and demands of the Law.)

The recent death of the Reverend Dr. Hans Herbert
Kramm, pastor of the historic St. John Church of Lüneburg, was noted by many friends in England and America. Dr. Kramm had served in England as a German
Lutheran pastor for seventeen years, during which time
he had also published several works on Luther in English. Dr. Kramm found an amazing lack of information about Martin Luther in England, not only among
the lay people, but even among the theologians. He was
asked such questions as these: "Do Lutheran churches
have altars? Do the Lutherans even have regularly-
installed pastors?" One Englishman, when told that
Kramm was a Lutheran, said at once: "Lutheran? Oh,
I know. Those are the people who change the Bible!"

How can one explain such ignorance and misconception? There have been many factors at work in England
which could partially explain this prejudice. But Kramm

said that one of the things which prevented the English from coming to an appreciation for Luther was the fact that they had restricted themselves to reading the young Luther! Kramm reported that the typical British student of theology read no more from Luther than the three reform treatises of 1520, as he found them in the Wace-Buchheim translation of 1896. Thus they had confined themselves to certain points of view that Luther had expressed in his formative years when he was using almost radical means to combat the problems that lay before him. Certain passages from these early writings of Luther had left the impression that Luther was a sort of Quaker or Enthusiast. It was in this way that the English had acquired their grotesque picture of Luther.[28]

So warped an understanding of Luther is not limited to England, but is found in many places. It should teach us that we cannot satisfy ourselves with merely one part of his career, whether that of the young or the mature Luther, but that we need to study his life and work in every period in relationship to the times in which he lived, and with regard to his associations with Melanchthon and other friends and co-workers. And so our program must be: Not alone the young Luther, not alone the elder Luther, not just a part of Luther, but the whole Luther, *Der ganze Kerl!*

---

[28]Hans-Herbert Kramm, "Luthers Wirkung heute in Grossbritannien," in *Luther* 26 (1955) 29 f.

Melanchthon in His Relation to Luther

IT IS with mixed feelings that I approach the task of speaking about Philip Melanchthon. On the one hand, it cannot be denied that our understanding of Luther's development is considerably hindered by our lack of knowledge about Melanchthon. On the other hand, the name of Melanchthon has been subjected to so much reproach that one has his misgivings about entering into the fray.

It was not enough that the first name of Luther's fellow reformer was attached in the sixteenth century to the Crypto-Calvinist movement, which was unjustly called "Philippism"; in the nineteenth century, when that regrettable movement called "American Lutheranism" brought forth a serious compromising of Evangelical Lutheran principles, the name "Melanchthonianism" was applied to the teachings of the party which fostered a platform that was inimical to true Lutheranism.[1] Even today, some Luther writers persist in calling errorists

---

[1] See Harold H. Lentz, *Reformation Crossroads: A Comparison of the Theology of Luther and Melanchthon.* Minneapolis, 1958, p. 8.

"Melanchthonianists." Often the strongest abuse against the name of Melanchthon comes from just those quarters where men claim to be the true representatives of the theology of the Augsburg Confession of 1530, a document written by none other than Philip Melanchthon. This aversion to the writer of the Augsburg Confession was further fostered through the medium of the recent film on Martin Luther, in which Melanchthon appeared to be a sort of feeble pedant who only accidentally got involved in the story of the Augsburg Confession. In the film that primary symbol of Evangelical Lutheranism was written in spite of Melanchthon rather than by him.

Any who hold this widely accepted view might well be amazed at the lofty praise that the friar of Wittenberg heaped upon his new young friend after Melanchthon's arrival at the university. Luther's admiration for Melanchthon once found expression in the well-known epigram, written on the table in chalk: "Substance and words, Philip; words without substance, Erasmus; substance without words, Luther; neither substance nor words, Carlstadt."[2] Luther regarded Melanchthon's *Loci communes* so highly that he declared it should be held second only to the Holy Scriptures, and was worthy of canonization![3]

What are we to say, in view of Luther's high esteem for Philip Melanchthon, about the subsequent discredit into which his name has fallen? Was Luther so poor a judge of character, and are Melanchthon's critics so able to look into the heart of man that we should follow them? The answer can be arrived at only by attempting to retrace the problem in the original sources. We cannot begin to study Melanchthon until we rid ourselves

[2]WA Tr. 3, No. 3619.
[3]WA xviii, 601.

of our prejudices and give him the chance to speak for himself. This is the first rule, surely, in scientific research: that we leave our prejudices behind and try to listen objectively to the evidence. If we study Melanchthon in this manner, it is true that we shall find some blemishes in his character, for Melanchthon was a sinner like the rest of the race. But we shall also discover that many charges leveled against him have been either untrue or else greatly exaggerated. Such examination will lead us to a new perspective of the problem of the relation between Luther and Melanchthon. In the short hour before us we cannot begin to solve this problem; we shall be able only to review some of the more obvious aspects of the relationship of these two men.

1. *The Present State of Melanchthon Research*

With no more baggage than a knapsack, Nikolaus Mueller wandered back and forth throughout Germany, seeking lost or hidden Melanchthoniana. With an amazing knack for discovery, Mueller was able to track down many long-lost letters and papers, and finally had added nearly a thousand items to the known writings of Melanchthon. When the lonely scholar died in 1912, his treasure was found hoarded under his bed.

The student of Melanchthon must still journey about in search of the sources needed for his study. The principal collection of Melanchthon's works is in the *Corpus Reformatorum,* where it occupies the first twenty-eight volumes. This work, which appeared more than a century ago, is sadly outdated. Not only is it incomplete, but the works that have been included are often given in inferior renderings.[4] Nevertheless these volumes are still indis-

---

[4]See the imposing collection of errors listed by Nikolaus Mueller, "Die Wittenberger Bewegung," as found in the *Archiv für Reformationsgeschichte*, VI, VII, and VIII (1907-1908).

pensable to the scholar of the Reformation. Otto Clemen attempted to fill in the gaps with a supplement to the *Corpus Reformatorum*. The parts that he and his co-workers completed are excellent, but the task was never finished. Other writers, including pre-eminently Karl Hartfelder and Theodor Kolde, prepared additional supplements, which are excellent as far as they go. More recently a new edition of Melanchthon's works has been begun under the editorship of Robert Stupperich. In spite of some unevenness in quality, this work is of vital significance. But it is no more than a student edition, presenting only a small selection of the more important writings. What is needed is a new comprehensive edition, prepared with the same care as the Weimar Edition of Luther's *Works*. With the publication of Luther's exegetical lectures, a new era opened up in Luther research. There are a number of similar lectures delivered by Melanchthon in his early years at Wittenberg which have not been published since the time of the Reformation. Their publication could open up new vistas in the study of the history of the Reformation. Today it is necessary to travel to the great libraries of Germany to gain access to some of these works, such as Melanchthon's lectures on Romans, Matthew and I and II Corinthians. Even in Germany, the center of Reformation research, these important works have been largely overlooked. The door is wide open for new discoveries in the life and work of Philip Melanchthon.

If the situation is lamentable in regard to the sources for studying Melanchthon, it is even worse with respect to the secondary literature. Literature on Melanchthon is surprisingly scarce, and most of it is weighted down with prejudices and preconceived ideas. In some rare instances the prejudice is favorable to Melanchthon, as in the case of one recent biography where Melanchthon is held up even to Luther's disadvantage.⁵ But ordinarily the treatment of Melanchthon is negative. Two charges are commonly made by writers on Melanchthon, and oddly enough, the two judgments, while mutually contradictory, are frequently held by the same writer. The first charge is that Melanchthon had no originality, and that he was only the mouthpiece for Luther; the second is that he had too much originality, and that he deviated too widely from the opinions of Luther and corrupted his teachings. Just why Melanchthon was supposed to agree completely with Luther has never been made clear. Has it ever been customary or desirable for two colleagues on a university faculty of theology to be carbon copies, the one of the other? And in our time it is important to remember that it is not Luther's private writings which have symbolical significance, but the Lutheran confessions as they are found in the Book of Concord. Certainly Luther himself never thought of his works as invested with timeless confessional character.

Most of the charges leveled against Melanchthon cannot be investigated or gainsaid, simply because they are not specific and cannot be tested in the light of the evidence. Another characteristic of negative criticism of Melanchthon is that it reflects conclusions drawn on the basis of secondary literature rather than of primary sources.

One of the most vehement literary antagonists of Melanchthon in our times has been Karl Holl, the great Luther scholar. Holl describes Melanchthon's theology frequently enough, but he does so in a slanted manner: too many adjectives and too few footnotes. For example, Holl asserts, typically, "Melanchthon corrupted the Lutheran

---

⁵Clyde Manschreck, *Melanchthon the Quiet Reformer*. New York, 1958.

doctrine of justification," meaning that he had not stayed with Luther's early analytic view, but had instead developed another form of justification.[6] Instead of grounding this statement in Melanchthon's own works, Holl says that he has read this in a book by Emanuel Hirsch! If the reader, anxious to trace this matter back, turns to Hirsch, he will find Melanchthon described in most abusive terms. But again the reader is disappointed to discover that the author exhibits no direct acquaintance with Melanchthon's writings. He admits, indeed, that "in my judgment on the relation between Melanchthon and Luther, I have for the most part only summarized the findings of earlier research."[7]

One may grant that Holl and Hirsch are excellent historians and writers, but has the time not come when theologians make a fresh study of Melanchthon by examining the evidence impartially rather than by collecting skeletons from old closets and by proceeding on conclusions predetermined without fair investigation?

One of the few writers who has succeeded in approaching Melanchthon with objectivity has been Werner Elert. Elert disliked intensely certain elements in Melanchthon's character, such as his excessive inclination to yield for the sake of peace. He disliked even more the areas of theology where Melanchthon was at his weakest, such as the doctrine of the Lord's Supper, his teaching on conversion, or his views on works and the Law. Yet Elert succeeded in giving Melanchthon a favorable evaluation such as few others have before or since.

---

[6]Holl I, 128.

[7]Emanuel Hirsch, *Die Theologie des Andreas Osiander und ihre geschichtlichen Voraussetzungen* Göttingen, 1919, p. 228 ff. The quotation is from p. 229. Jaroslav Pelikan, *From Luther to Kierkegaard: A Study in the History of Theology.* St. Louis, 1950, 153, f.n. 110, etc., also cites Hirsch as authoritative.

His essay, "Humanity and the Church," prepared for the observance of the 450th birthday of Melanchthon in 1947, offers one of the most enlightening of discussions on the problem of Melanchthon and Luther. With particular reference to the postwar situation in Germany, Elert writes:

> What Melanchthon has meant theologically has often enough been investigated. But there is not one single presentation that does not let him appear completely overshadowed by Luther. This is true even of Melanchthon's opinion of himself. "I learned the Gospel from him," he confesses in his testament of 1540. But the other question, whether on the other hand Luther might also have learned from Melanchthon in theological matters, has until now never been raised, let alone answered. It appears to us that this approach could yield very important results for tracing the development of Luther's concept of the church, as well as for his doctrine of justification and the proper relation between Law and Gospel.[8]

The attitudes which Elert here calls for are basic to all sound scholarship. As he indicates, there is a vast amount of work yet to be done in this area of research.

2. Melanchthon's Development Before His Coming to Wittenberg

Psychologists have shown us the significance of one's childhood experiences for one's future growth. We are fortunate that the childhood of Luther has been carefully investigated, particularly in Otto Scheel's substantial two-volume work on Luther's early years. With Luther the task has been complicated through the accretion of ill-substantiated but persistent legends. In the case of Melanchthon's childhood, there are comparatively

---

[8] Werner Elert, "Humanität und Kirche: Zum 450. Geburtstag Melanchthons," in *Zwischen Gnade und Ungnade*, etc. München, 1948, 96.

few such tales that need to be debunked, and yet it must be said that no thorough investigation utilizing modern methods of historical research has ever been made of Melanchthon's early years. It is clear that the Melanchthon who came to Wittenberg in 1518 must be understood in continuity with the boy who was born twenty-one years earlier, who developed under certain specific conditions, who received a certain type of education, and who had therefore reached certain stages in his development before he met Luther. The fact that much of this is unknown is a major obstacle to our understanding of Melanchthon and Luther in their mutual relationship. It places a challenging task before historical theology for many years to come.

Melanchthon was born in 1497 at Bretten, a small town in southwestern Germany, located within the diocese of Speyer, and situated midway between Heidelberg and Stuttgart. His parents were pious people, devoted to the Church. His father was a skilled smith, having made armor for the nobility, the king, and even for the emperor. His mother came from a brilliant family, being a niece of the celebrated humanist, Johann Reuchlin. The family name was actually Schwartzerd or Schwartzert, but Reuchlin, as a compliment to his brilliant grand-nephew, had translated his name into the Greek word *Melanchthon,* which means "black earth," under the erroneous impression that this was a proper rendering of the German. Although the father died when Philip was very young, the boy was given the best possible education. First he enjoyed a private tutor, and then was sent to the fine Latin school conducted at Pforzheim by Georg Simler and Johannes Hildebrandt.[9]

When Melanchthon was only twelve years old he en-

---

[9] CR 10, 258 f.

rolled at the University of Heidelberg, where he received
the Bachelor of Arts degree three years later. He stayed
on at Heidelberg, soon fulfilling the requirements for the
master's degree. Learning that he was to be rejected
because of his youth, however, Melanchthon left the university town on the Neckar to visit the university at
Tübingen. He remained at Tübingen for approximately
six years, after which he moved to Wittenberg, where
he remained for the rest of his life.

The faculty at Heidelberg was apparently rather me-
diocre at the time Melanchthon studied there. The school
was basking in the glory of a quarter century earlier,
when the humanist Rudolph Agricola had taught there
and gathered about himself an imposing group of brilliant men including Reuchlin. During his student days
Melanchthon read the works of Agricola assiduously. The
influence of Agricola remained upon Melanchthon for
the rest of his life and was one of the decisive factors
in his being led into the humanist camp.[10] At Heidelberg
Melanchthon had the opportunity of meeting the famed
humanist Jacob Wimpfeling who was visiting there at
the time. Wimpfeling was a friend of the Strassburg
preacher Johann Geiler von Kaisersberg. Together these
two men had edited and published the writings of John
Gerson, the Occamist and mystic of the preceding century. Melanchthon became very much interested in Geiler,
who was a fiery preacher and desirous of churchly reform.
When Geiler died in 1510, Melanchthon wrote his first
poem, a eulogy which was incorporated by Wimpfeling
into a memorial volume for Geiler.

In spite of his connections with such humanists as

[10]See Melanchthon's preface to the new edition of Agricola's *Lucubra-
tiones*, CR 3, 673 ff. Cf. Karl Hartfelder, *Philip Melanchthon als Praeceptor Germaniae.* Berlin, 1889 (Monumenta Germaniae paedagogica.
bd. VII) 19 f.

Reuchlin, Geiler, and Wimpfeling, it is significant to note that when Melanchthon was graduated with the bachelor's degree, his name was not listed among the Occamists or followers of the *via moderna,* but among the followers of Thomas, those of the *via antiqua.* Behind this designation lay the influence of Pallas Spangel. Although Spangel as a pupil of Agricola had espoused the cause of Humanism, he remained true to the thought world of Aquinas. Spangel saw in Humanism nothing more than a means for making the old truths more palatable for a new age.[11] It is puzzling to note that only a few months after Melanchthon had received the bachelor's degree as a Thomist, he joined the ranks of the Occamists at Tübingen. While at Tübingen, Melanchthon busied himself in studying the works of John Gerson and of Johann Wessel, also of Nominalist philosophical persuasion and an early teacher of Reuchlin. At this time he also worked in the printshop of Thomas Anshelm as proof-reader. While he was engaged in correcting the *Chronicles* of Johann Nauclerus, an event took place which led to Melanchthon's getting a copy of the Bible. Melanchthon's friends related this incident:

Since the first part was badly confused, he had to bring it into order and make corrections, which he could not do without the Bible. But at that time it was hard to get a copy of the Bible. Nevertheless he finally got a small Bible, which he read industriously day and night. Thereby he won a strong interest in theology, which led him to hear the theological lectures, while he studied the Greek and Hebrew languages on the side.[12]

This evidence would seem to indicate that, contrary to general opinion, Melanchthon was already a student

---

[11] See Hartfelder, 18-21

[12] This incident is related by Melanchthon's colleagues in a biography prepared by them after his death. CR 10, 260.

of the Bible before he came to Wittenberg. Another report has it that Melanchthon as a student at Tübingen
was criticized for having sat in church reading the Bible
during the saying of the Mass. Another indication of
Melanchthon's early interest in the Holy Scriptures would
be the fact that immediately upon his arrival at Wittenberg he announced that he was going to give lectures
on the Bible. This would presuppose a considerable acquaintance with the Scriptures. The common assertion
that Melanchthon came to Wittenberg without ever having heard of Luther and ignorant of the movement
emerging under Luther's leadership would also appear
to be contrary to probability. It is inconceivable that
while all Germany was astir over the Ninety-five Theses
of Luther the previous year, Melanchthon should have
been so ill-informed of current events from his place
at Tübingen.

Much work remains to be done to reconstruct more
adequately Melanchthon's early life. In particular, the
extent of Melanchthon's indebtedness to Agricola, Gerson, Wessel, and Geiler needs further clarification, and
his relationship to medieval philosophy as a whole is a
problem which has scarcely been touched upon.

3. *Melanchthon and Luther as Friends and Co-workers*

On August 29, 1518, Melanchthon delivered his inaugural address in the Castle Church at Wittenberg. He
spoke of the need for a renewal of learning, and pointed
his hearers to the importance of primary sources. Among
his fascinated listeners sat Martin Luther. A few days
later crowds of students sat at his feet for instruction
in Greek. Among those who had come to learn was
Martin Luther. Letters written by both men to their
acquaintances show that a friendship sprang up in those

143

days which was to become famous in the annals of the Reformation. But there is a question which ought to be asked: Did these two men remain close friends all their lives? It is usually taken for granted that they both had the same regard for each other as long as they lived. It is true that they remained co-workers. But the quality and closeness of their relationship is quite a different matter.

In one of the best treatises on the relationship between Melanchthon and Luther, Gustav Mix divided their association into three periods. Since his essay was based on authentic and carefully evaluated sources, his findings are worthy of careful consideration. The first period Mix dates from 1518 to 1521. In 1522, when Luther strongly rebuked Melanchthon for his lack of leadership in the Wittenberg disturbance of the previous year, Melanchthon became offended, so that their friendship was by no means as close between 1522 and 1527. As Mix observed, Melanchthon no longer called Luther his "dearest friend Martin," *amicissimus Martinus,* but began to address him rather coolly as "Reverend Father." Luther did not succeed in overcoming his resentment until 1527, when Melanchthon's son died. In this crisis, Luther's solicitude and tender understanding so helped Melanchthon that their friendship was restored and endured until Luther's death in 1546, although it was never again as hearty as during the first three years.[13]

Mix's analysis rings true to the facts as I find them in my study of the relation between the two reformers. It is of great significance to note that under the impact of Luther's personality, Melanchthon, who had come to Wittenberg with the resolve to publish a new edition

---

[13]Gustav Mix, "Luther und Melanchthon in ihrer gegenseitigen Beurteilung," in *Theologische Studien und Kritiken,* 74 (1901) 482 f.

of Aristotle's works, turned his back on philosophy for a time. It is also clear that in theological matters he was, for the most part, a grateful pupil of Luther even though there were many areas in which Luther also learned from Melanchthon. Nevertheless after 1522 Melanchthon returned to philosophy and began to go his own way in theology. After 1527, although many instances of a renewal of their friendship may be observed, it is significant to note that while Luther called Melanchthon by his first name, Melanchthon respectfully addressed him as Dr. Luther.[14]

4. The Divergence

The year 1521 was a fateful year for the cause of the evangelical reformation. It was the year of Luther's heroic stand at Worms, the year of his enforced confinement at the Wartburg, a year in which new responsibilities were placed into the hands of Melanchthon, the year of the appearance of the first Lutheran dogmatics, Melanchthon's *Loci communes,* and the year during which revolutionaries brought the town of Wittenberg into great unrest and to the brink of bloodshed. The turn that the Reformation took at Wittenberg in that year offered a testing of the positions previously

[14]An interesting account of the relations between Melanchthon and Luther has been left by Ratzeberger. An eye-witness, Ratzeberger claimed that Melanchthon was secretly resentful of Luther, believing that Luther was trying to make a name for himself and that Luther did not want any rival to gain recognition. Ratzeberger wrote that Melanchthon's friends, instead of encouraging him to put a good construction on Luther's actions, incited him to greater suspicion, presumably in order to endear themselves to Melanchthon. This report is interesting enough, but it is to be used with caution, since Ratzeberger was a notorious enemy of Melanchthon, and sought to discredit him in other ways. See Matthäus Ratzeberger, *Die Handschriftliche Geschichte Ratzebergers über Luther und seine Zeit,* hrsg. von d. Chr. Gotth. Neudecker. Jena, 1850, 88.

taken by both Luther and Melanchthon. The next few years were to usher in the period of the mature Reformation.

Twice in his lifetime, in 1521 and in 1546, the leadership of the Reformation was placed in Melanchthon's hands. Both times he proved unequal to the task. Melanchthon was a great scholar and organizer, but he did not have the heroic qualities of leadership that Luther possessed. Both men had pointed out the abuses in the old church. They had denounced the practices associated with Holy Communion, they had spoken against the abuses of monasticism, and they had denied the authority of hierarchy. Especially in his reform treatise "On the Freedom of the Christian Man," Luther had impressively taught that the Christian is a free man, subject to none. But Luther had been slow to introduce reform because he felt that the people were not yet ready for it, and he feared it would bring offense to tender consciences. The other part of his paradox on Christian liberty therefore prevailed: the Christian man is a slave, and in bondage to all, through the law of love. During his year at the Wartburg, this second part of the paradox was forgotten by many, with serious consequences.

The disturbances at Wittenberg began when radical men began to demand an immediate end to existing conditions and a prompt introduction of reformational practices and teachings. At the head of the movement in the fall of 1521 stood Gabriel Zwilling, a brother monk of Luther in the Augustinian monastery.[15] Zwilling

---

[15] The sources for the Wittenberg disturbances have been admirably collected and annotated by Nikolaus Mueller, *op. cit.* An interesting monograph covering the period is that by Hermann Barge, *Andreas Bodenstein von Karlstadt.* Leipzig, 1905.

took Luther's place as preacher while the latter was absent, and seems to have appointed himself to take over the reins of the Reformation as well. The monastery chapel enjoyed a good attendance of the townsfolk at the services, and Zwilling opportunistically stirred up the people to a zeal for radical reform. On September 29 Melanchthon, together with his students, received the Lord's Supper in both kinds. Although this was a great departure from custom, the service seems to have been of semi-private nature and it appears that the practice was not soon repeated.[16] Apparently the first public celebration of the Sacrament according to evangelical usage was in Carlstadt's Christmas Day service of 1521. This celebration grew out of a bitter controversy Carlstadt had with the conservative chapter members; because of this, the celebration had been forbidden by the Elector Frederick the Wise. When Carlstadt persisted in his intent to hold the service, wild demonstrations from the public the night before proclaimed the innovations. Crowds thronged through the parish church, singing coarse songs, threatening the priests, and damaging the furnishings. On the following day, Carlstadt held the first public Communion service according to reformational principles, supplemented by a few notions of his own. Dressed in his everyday clothes, Carlstadt preached a sermon in which he denounced previous abuses, then proceeded to the Sacrament. The Communion was celebrated with

---

[16]This is based on a letter of the student, Sebastian Helmann, to Johann Hess, written from Wittenberg on October 8: "Verbum dei fideliter audimus, demum sub una specie non communicamus, sed vtranque capimus, et id sepe nobis continget. Philippus Melanchton cum omnibus suis discipulis in parrochia in die Michaelis sub Vtraque specie communicauit, et iam fiet in omnibus." Mueller, *op. cit.*, VI, 177. The statement that Communion in both kinds had become customary does not harmonize with the events of December of that year, and must seemingly be ascribed to youthful exaggeration.

a liturgy sharply pruned of offensive elements, the climax of which was the giving of both the bread and the wine to the laity.[17]

Meanwhile other great disturbances had shaken the tranquility of Wittenberg. From a nearby town appeared three men who came to be known as the "Zwickau prophets," Nicholas Storch, Thomas Marx, and Mark Stübner. They brought with them strange doctrines based on their private interpretation of the Bible and claimed also to have direct revelations from God in the form of visions and dreams. They denounced many of the former teachings and practices of the old church, denied the right to baptize infants, insisted on the destruction of images in the churches, and taught that it was unscriptural to hold or attend schools, since Jesus had forbidden His disciples to be addressed as teachers. The result was that many talented students left the university and went home to learn a trade. Even Carlstadt was misled by these strange prophets, and wandered about the streets of Wittenberg, asking the simple folk to explain to him obscure passages of the Bible.[18] This movement spelled the defeat of the educational system. Melanchthon was beside himself; he did not know how to answer these Enthusiasts.[19]

The scorn that the Enthusiasts held for education was part of a feeling quite general throughout Germany at that time, with grievous consequences for the universities. At Wittenberg the enrollment dropped sharply. Whereas between the Easters of 1520 and 1521, 579

[17]See Barge, 357 ff.

[18]The source is Froeschel's Preface, as given in B. J. Kidd, *Documents Illustrative of the Continental Reformation.* Oxford, 1911, 103 f.

[19]The interesting account which relates how Melanchthon finally realized that Stübner was a fraud is given by the contemporary biographer, Joachim Camerarius, in *De Vita P. Melanchthonis. . .* Halle, 1777, 51 f.

new students had enrolled, the number fell in the next three years to 245, 285, and 197. A glance at the University *Album,* which recorded the names of all students and teachers entering the institution, indicates that during the next ten years the school more than once was at the point of closing its doors. From 1524 until 1532 not a single candidate applied for the doctorate in theology.[20] The situation was acute not only at Wittenberg, but all over Germany. Between 1521 and 1525, the total annual matriculations at eleven universities sank from 1708 to 652. The University of Greifswald was closed from 1525 until 1539, while the University of Rostock received a low of nine new students in 1526.[21] As was to be expected, the Reformation got much of the blame, particularly from the Catholics, for this educational catastrophe. As a matter of fact, it was clear that fanatical elements of the Reformation were dangerously hostile to the furtherance of learning and to the future of the educational institutions.

This crisis seems to have worked a profound effect in the thinking of Melanchthon. As a Biblical humanist, he had joined with Luther in blaming tradition and in limiting the sphere of reason. The dangerous situation in the educational world pointed out a weakness in their thinking. Biblicism in itself could not guarantee evangelical liberty. Since biblicism consisted of an approach to the Bible without due regard for historical development, it carried with it an excessive individualism. This individualism in turn was all too ready to fall back into the

---

[20]See Wittenberg University's reissue of *Album academiae Vitebergensis,* . . . Leipzig, 1841, I. See also Walter Friedensburg, *Urkundenbuch der Universität Wittenberg.* Vol. I, Magdeburg, 1926, I, and his *Geschichte der Universität Wittenberg.* Halle, 1917. The crisis of 1522 is also discussed in Peter Petersen, *Geschichte der Aristotelischen Philosophie im Protestantischen Deutschland.* Leipzig, 1921, 40.

[21]Barge, 419.

error of legalism. It became increasingly clear to Melanchthon that the new church had to benefit from a learning established upon a broader base than that of a narrow biblicism.

It was at this point that he discovered what was to become his life's calling. It was to be his task to press the liberal arts into the service of the Gospel, relating the older learning to the new reformational insights. The humanities also were needed to defend Christian liberty. By educating in the humanities future theologians, parish preachers, lawyers, physicians, and other leaders, Melanchthon was to endeavor to provide them with an adequate frame of reference in which they might develop their Christian freedom and in turn communicate the precious truths of the Gospel to others. This became his answer to the threat of obscurantist Enthusiasm, as it manifested itself in its destructiveness in the terror-laden year of 1521-1522 at Wittenberg.[22]

Melanchthon's concern for orderliness seems to have gradually led him into a certain kind of legalism. Writings from 1521 already show a new prominence of the Law, which gradually led to his doctrine of the third use of the Law. He became increasingly suspicious of his earlier doctrine of predestination and election, and sought to make more room for human responsibility. Thus the year 1522 is the time from which to date the divergence between Melanchthon and Luther. Accompanying the perplexities of 1522 was a rift between the two men which went back to Luther's sharpness in criticizing Melanchthon for not having ruled with a firmer hand during his year of absence. Even though the friendship was restored in later years, a divergency which was to remain permanent gradually developed and was made

---

[22]See Elert, 92 ff.

evident in their teachings. Luther tended to emphasize the work of God in men's salvation, while Melanchthon stressed human responsibility. Luther stressed the Real Presence in Holy Communion; and although Melanchthon shared Luther's Christological presuppositions, he was often unclear on the nature of the presence of the Lord in His Supper. Through the years, minor misunderstandings clouded their association from time to time. Yet they remained close co-workers, for even on the occasions when Melanchthon felt that he had been insulted by Luther, he always regarded him as the prophet sent of God to reform the Church, and he was willing to subordinate himself to Luther. In spite of the divergencies of their teaching, they remained in essential doctrinal unity until their relation was ended by Luther's death in 1546.

5. *The Elder Melanchthon Without Luther*

It was the misfortune of Melanchthon's life that Luther preceded him in death. The troubled political events of the next five years would have been a sore test even of Luther's stalwart leadership. To the gentle Melanchthon they brought problems with which he was simply unfitted to cope. For many years previous to Luther's death, men who counted themselves among Luther's friends and Melanchthon's enemies had sought to destroy their relationship, but in vain. Melanchthon's unfortunate experience in politics, when though he had rejected a compromise with the papists at the time of the Augsburg Interim, he later compromised in halfheartedly endorsing the Leipzig Interim, brought down upon him the resentment of a large part of the Lutheran Church at a time when many members of his church were bravely facing persecution.

151

One of the greatest causes of dissatisfaction with Melanchthon came as the result of his celebrated letter to Carlowitz, written on April 28, 1548. In it he wrote that during the lifetime of Luther he had yielded many times for the sake of peace, since there was no principle involved, but that if he were asked to yield now to the papists he would have to refuse, regardless of any personal consequences. The part that aroused the ire of the Lutherans was this indiscreet sentence: "Formerly I bore an unseemly servitude to Luther, when in many instances he was guided by his quarrelsome moods, in which he aided neither his own reputation nor the public welfare."[23] Carlowitz published this letter, which of course enjoyed wide circulation, and stirred up a popular anger which Melanchthon never completely succeeded in living down. We may readily believe that Luther, who is known to have been rather cantankerous in his later years, was occasionally a trial to the mild-mannered Melanchthon. But it was very unwise of him to share so partial and ill-considered a judgment with the treacherous Carlowitz. Through this and other unfortunate experiences which clouded the last years of Melanchthon's life, controversies resulted which later threatened the peace of the Lutheran Church. Certain followers of Melanchthon became secret promoters of Calvinistic ideas. Although there is no evidence that Melanchthon was in any way a Crypto-Calvinist, the movement became known in history as "Philippism." The result has been that the name of Philip Melanchthon has been regarded with deep suspicion by those who wanted to be most loyal to the Holy Scriptures and the confessional books of the Evangelical Lutheran Church.

[23]CR 6, 880. See also the analysis and defense of Melanchthon in Manschreck, 279 ff.

We cannot condone Melanchthon's mistakes, nor can we endorse his doctrine where he was in error. Nevertheless the tendency which has existed for more than four centuries to ignore his contribution has retarded rather than aided our quest for the meaning of true Lutheranism. Philip Melanchthon, as perhaps no other prominent man from the Reformation, is a living example of Luther's great paradox: that the Christian believer is *simul justus et peccator*, at the same time a righteous man and a sinner. And rather than heap criticism upon this frail and yet effective instrument in the hand of God, it behooves us to approach our study of this man with humility and charity.

Martin Luther was the son of a miner, and Philip Melanchthon was the son of a smith. The occupations of their fathers are an analogy of the relationship which they bore to one another in the Reformation. It was Luther, the miner's son, who dug deeply to extract the ore that was hidden from the view of his contemporaries. And it was Melanchthon, the son of the smith, who worked the raw material into a finished and organized system. They stood together, the son of the miner and the son of the smith. Left to their own human resources, they were weak. But under God, they formed a team through which the pure light of the Gospel was rediscovered and sent forth into the world.

The Renaissance in Lutheran Theology

D OES Martin Luther have a message for the Church today? Some would say flatly, "No! Luther belongs to an age now past. It is a dangerous attitude when one looks to the past for his answers." There are those in our land today who are belittling Luther research as an aspect of "Neo-Orthodoxy" which they regard as involving an undue dependence upon the past. In other quarters one senses a silent hostility toward Luther research which expresses itself in a more passive type of resistance. And the educational system in this country, with its ties to the philosophy of John Dewey, and the consequent decline in foreign language study, has made it increasingly difficult to provide a college or seminary education which gives the student the ability to do independent study in Luther or in the Confessions.

Does Martin Luther have a message for the Church today? This same question was answered with a No! in the land of the Reformation 150 years ago. Rationalism had come close to stilling the voice of the Gospel. Participation in the life of the Church had nearly died out

154

in many parts of Germany and Scandinavia. It is important for us to note that our Lutheran brethren in Europe did not recover from their theological lethargy until the movement called the "Luther renaissance" got under way. At that time, men learned to their surprise that although Luther had been dead for hundreds of years, he did have a message for the Church. When Biblical theology had become more and more negative in its analysis of the four gospels, it was in large measure the new studies in Luther which brought the Gospel back to the Church in Germany, Sweden, and other countries.

The story of the Luther renaissance reads like an exciting novel. Among the forerunners were men like von Hofmann and Theodosius Harnack. The Weimar Edition of Luther's *Works*, edited with a precision made possible by the application of new methods in critical work in sources, was a necessary prerequisite. The discovery of the early lectures of Luther gave the movement tremendous impetus. Carl Stange is credited with having directed the attention of scholars to the importance of these Latin works of Luther. Karl Holl deserves special mention for his outstanding studies in the young Luther. Johannes von Walter was one of the few scholars of his time who recognized that not only the young Luther, but also the mature Luther must be thoroughly studied. Soon Germany had many outstanding men doing research in Luther and making important discoveries. Methods of scientific historical research were applied and yielded impressive results. The older men were joined by men like Scheel, Hirsch, Vogelsang, and Boehmer in Germany; while in Sweden a new galaxy of names such as Bring, Aulén, and Nygren carried on the movement in the north. J. Michael Reu of Dubuque, Iowa, represented an important link between Europe and America in Luther study. Younger men joined the ranks of European scholars: Althaus, Elert, Bornkamm, Maurer, Sasse, Wingren, and others. In America and England they were joined by such Lutherans as Preus, Tappert, Schwiebert, Pelikan, Grimm, Quanbeck, and Saarnivaara. Unexpected reinforcements came from non-Lutherans on both sides of the Atlantic: Rupp, Watson, and Bainton, to mention only the most prominent.

Thus the Luther renaissance is beginning to make itself felt also in Anglo-Saxon lands. Certainly the 1957 Minneapolis Assembly of the Lutheran World Federation provided considerable incentive. Americans with the grace of self-examination learned much from their European brethren. It became clearer than ever that Lutheran theology in this country still had a long way to go. The decision to devote the next five years to an emphasis of the Lutheran Confessions should be particularly helpful to the American section.[1] Lutherans in America are in a particularly difficult position with regard to theology. There is no Lutheran university which has succeeded in establishing itself in offering recognized graduate work in all the branches of learning, particularly theology. Graduate schools with Calvinistic or other traditions have graciously accepted Lutheran students. While the hospitality of these institutions deserves our appreciation, we cannot expect them to solve our theological problems. It remains the task of the Lutheran Church in America to teach and write a theology which will win the re-

---

[1] It is significant that this decision should have come at a time when the American Lutheran Church, the United Lutheran Church, the Suomi Synod, and the Augustana Lutheran Church were engaged in union negotiations in which they watered down their subscription to the Confessions. Such a move weakens the ties to ecumenical Lutheranism. It is to be hoped that this lost ground will be recovered in the future.

spect of others and will meet the problems that the twentieth century has presented.

It is exactly at this point that we wish to affirm our conviction that Martin Luther does indeed have a message for the Church today, and particularly for American Lutheranism, still only the third largest non-Roman denomination. But a word of caution is in order. Our watchword dare not be "Back to Luther"; it must rather be "Forward with Luther!" A mere repristinary method which regards Luther as an oracle of advice for every situation will quickly slip into a new scholasticism. Theological development did not end with Luther, nor does he have the answer to every question that arises today. We need no mechanical repristination, but rather a vital renaissance. Luther is to be studied not simply in order that he may slavishly be followed, but because he preaches the Gospel. From him we may learn to become more faithful soldiers of the Cross.

Another cautionary note may be sounded. In America, the writings of Luther and the Confessions have sometimes been used legalistically. Too often they have been used to accuse others of unfaithfulness to the truth; in such instances, their use has been related to the Law rather than to the Gospel. We cannot permit such misuse of Luther in the past to discourage us from the benefits of Luther study today, nor can we allow ourselves the luxury of a polemical misuse which sometimes characterized the past. But under proper premises, this study can enrich us immeasurably, as it has our brethren in Germany and Scandinavia. A renaissance in Lutheran theology is already in evidence in this country. Luther has a message to give to the American church and her developing theology today.

In this my final lecture I shall first endeavor to make

specific some points at which Luther, Melanchthon, and others from the past can give us guidance today. Next I shall discuss our educational system and how it may more adequately provide the skills and knowledge necessary to original and fruitful research. Finally I shall discuss the methods of historical research appropriate to this kind of scholarship.

1. *What the Reformers Can Contribute to Our Theology Today*

There are many fundamental questions facing Lutheran theology in the United States. It will not be possible here to do more than to raise a few of these questions and indicate where Luther and his co-laborers may help us solve our problems.

The first major problem which demands clarification today is the relationship between theology and philosophy. It is significant that some prominent schools of theology in the United States offer courses in the philosophy of religion in the place of systematic theology. Modern confusion is illustrated in Paul Tillich's concept of "philosophical theology." In my judgment, this is a contradiction in terms. It is true that theology must be studied in its relation to philosophy, but what Tillich seems to be trying to do is to adjust theology to suit the demands of existentialist philosophy. Rudolf Bultmann is engrossed in the same attempt. For him, the problem is at least partly met in his brilliant commentary on St. John when he introduces his own philosophy with these characteristic words: "This passage must be understood existentially." But why? Is it not clear to anyone with a minimum of historical understanding that neither John, Paul, nor Jesus was a pupil of Kierkegaard, Heidegger, Sartre, or Jaspers? In spite of their important contributions, both Tillich and Bultmann are in danger of allowing their philosophy to become a world-view in which the Gospel is allowed to say only what is consistent with that world-view. The result no longer belongs to theology, but is rather a part of philosophy.

It would be too much to expect or even desire Luther or Melanchthon to provide us with a cut-and-dried philosophy for the twentieth century. But the basic principles upon which they met similar problems in their own time can nevertheless be most instructive for us. On the one hand, they recognized the limitations of philosophy in the service of the Gospel, and on the other, they were able to perceive where it could help.

Luther's negative judgments regarding certain philosophers are widely known. When we remember how the philosophy of Occam for a long time kept Luther from receiving the comfort of the Gospel, we are not surprised that he turned against Occam after the Gospel had become his own. Or when we consider the dependence upon Aristotle of the Roman theologians in their scholastic system, it ought not surprise us that Luther called Aristotle "the rancid philosopher," the story-teller, the destroyer of pious teaching, and the master of the heathen.[2] Luther showed that philosophy was limited because it depended on the powers of human reason and speculation. On the other hand, theology was based on God's revelation. Since spiritual truths could be taught only by the Holy Ghost, it was clear that philosophy should not invade the field of theology.[3] Largely because of Me-

---

[2] See Otto Scheel, *Dokumente zu Luthers Entwicklung*, Tübingen, 1911, Nos. 234, 253, 561, 553, 40, 344, etc.

[3] Luther's sharp delimiting of the powers of human reason has been offensive to some. An excellent answer to the objections of John Wesley and others is given by Philip S. Watson in *Let God Be God! An Interpretation of the Theology of Martin Luther*. Philadelphia, 1950, 86.

lanchthon's prompting, Luther was also willing to acknowledge that philosophy could be employed in the service of the Gospel, particularly in dialectics and rhetoric. This growing appreciation is more characteristic of the mature Luther than of the younger reformer[4]

Nevertheless it was to be expected that Melanchthon should make the greater contribution toward an understanding of the proper relationship between theology and philosophy. Melanchthon's own attitude to philosophy has never been thoroughly studied, and exaggerated claims have often been made as to the extent of his preoccupation with pure philosophy. Actually he seems to have been uninterested in the controversy over universals. To be sure, he was a member of the philosophy department at Wittenberg; but this department of the University was so broad as to correspond more closely to a liberal arts college than to a school of philosophy in our day. Certainly Melanchthon was at home in philosophy as well as in theology. Especially after the anarchy at Wittenberg in 1521-1522, Melanchthon regarded the humanities as an important leavening agent for the Reformation, and undertook to rehabilitate philosophy. He did so on the premise that philosophy could help provide the *form* for communicating the Gospel, but that it must not be allowed to change the *content*. Logic, dialectic, and rhetoric, as well as the languages, were placed in the service of the Reformation, so that pastors and lay workers might more effectively further the evangelical cause. Two generations of pastors and lay leaders received the stamp of Melanchthon's liberal arts emphases before going into their specialized professional training, and they then carried the Reforma-

---

[4]See his *Large Commentary on Galatians*, WA, xl, I, 410.

tion's message into their respective areas of influence in Germany, Scandinavia, and other European countries.

There is a tendency to find fault with Melanchthon for having provided the early Lutheran Church with a unified world-view modelled after the philosophy of Aristotle. Yet Melanchthon was doing no more than showing the relationship of the Word of God to the contemporary scene, and to do so he had to relate it to Aristotelianism, which was the most influential and usable philosophy of that time. Our own situation today stands in disadvantageously marked contrast to the splendid unity that existed between theology, music, literature, the plastic arts, and metaphysics during the age of Lutheran Orthodoxy. Those days cannot be recalled, but it ill becomes us to attack this achievement of a past age, while we ourselves develop a crazy-quilt of thought, in which theology, philosophy, literature, music, and art are intermingled in an incongruous way that has confused both ourselves and our non-Lutheran neighbors. We need philosophy indeed, but not borrowed finery—a philosophy rather which rises out of our own situation, which makes it a major concern to remain the servant of the Church, not to change or assume superiority over her proclamation.

The second major problem has to do with the right orientation of theology. Luther would teach us that God must stand at the center. Man's self-interest must be ruthlessly uprooted. It was of great concern to Luther to free theology from every trace of eudaemonism. True Christianity means that one's will is so completely conformed to the will of God that the Christian is willing to go to hell instead of heaven, should God will it (*resignatio ad infernos*). Melanchthon pointed out that self-love, *amor sui*, constitutes the essence of sin. The way of faith

161

is the way of the *theologia crucis,* which means denying oneself to take up the Cross and follow Jesus.[5]

This theocentric insight needs again to be reasserted in theology. Especially under the impact of Existentialism, man has once again been placed back in the center. Not God, but rather my ego, or God in His relation to my ego and subject to my apprehension of Him, stands at the center of the stage. Theology becomes the study of *my* ultimate concern. Any teaching about God which does not concern *me* loses its place in the theological system. Tillich goes as far as to say that ". . . God in His self-manifestation is dependent on the way man receives His manifestation."[6] Such a statement is thoroughly anthropocentric. God is made to revolve around man. Tillich seems to have left himself open to charges of what Anders Nygren calls the religion of *eros.*[7] Such an anthropocentric approach can be harmonized neither with the findings of Biblical theology nor with the historical concensus of the Church in her dogmas and theology. Not man's dilemma, but God's work must stand in the center. Not I, but Christ Jesus, and Him crucified.

Closely related to the theocentric emphasis in reformational theology is its Christocentric character. This was developed by Luther even in his earlier writings. Especially in his work on the Psalms in 1519 and the following years, and in his polemic against Latomus,

---

[5]Melanchthon's position can be traced as early as the *Theologica Institutio* of 1518: the delivery in CR 21 is poor but usable. Luther's *theologia crucis* is developed in the Heidelberg Disputation of 1518, WA I. A fine exposition of this is given by Walther von Loewenich, *Luthers Theologia crucis.* 45th ed., 1954.

[6]Paul Tillich, *Systematic Theology.* Chicago, 1953, I, 61.

[7]See Anders Nygren's important work, *Agape and Eros.* Philadelphia, 1953, 68 ff. Luther's theocentricism is discussed by Karl Holl in his essay, "Was verstand Luther unter Religion?" in his *Gesammelte Aufsätze,* 73 ff. Watson gives a fine discussion of this problem is his book, *Let God Be God,* 33 ff.

Luther showed the connection between incarnation and redemption.[8] The concept called the *frohlicher Wechsel*, that is, the joyful exchange in which Christ takes the sinner's burden and clothes him with His righteousness in return, helped to inform Lutheran thinking for centuries to come. One example of this is Johann Sebastian Bach's cantata, *Wachet auf! ruft uns die Stimme* (Wake, Awake! For Night Is Flying), where in a duet of matchless beauty and spiritual depth, the relation between the believer and Christ is portrayed. In Bach's "B-Minor Mass" the parallel construction of the *Incarnatus est* and the *Crucifixus est* also indicates that the continuity between incarnation and redemption was preserved in the age of Lutheran orthodoxy. When Gustaf Aulén makes charges to the contrary, he is simply overlooking a great deal of important material. And over against Aulén's accusations that Melanchthon failed to preserve this continuity, we may cite Melanchthon's own words as found in the Lectures on St. Matthew, too often ignored, which were delivered during his earliest years at Wittenberg:

> Moreover the whole argument of the Gospel is as follows: the incarnation of Christ, by which is proclaimed how God put on our flesh, and we put on God. . . . The summary of our salvation is that the Son of God clothed Himself in our flesh, and in the form of a man transferred our sin to Himself, that we, held under by sin, should not [be kept] by our sin. . . . Christ descended to the earth, taking the feeble nature of man, bearing sin, and imparting the Spirit of righteousness.[9]

[8] See Wilhelm Maurer's essay, "Die Einheit der Theologie Luthers," in *Theologische Literaturzeitung*, 75 (1950), Col. 245-252.

[9] This reference is taken from a source not published since the Reformation: *Philippi Melanchthonis in Euangelium Matthaei, iam recens in gratiam studiosorum editae* (1523), Fol. Aiij.

It was furthermore of utmost importance to Luther and Melanchthon to show that this Son of God who had taken on human nature had not departed from His own at the Ascension, but that according to both His divine and human natures He kept His promise: "Lo, I am with you alway." If we study some of the statements made by both men at the Colloquy of Marburg in 1529, as well as remarks in their letters and other writings, we discover that it was just this point which represented for them the crux of the matter in the discussions with Zwingli. The Reformed group which gathered about Zwingli maintained that the finite is not capable of containing the infinite *(finitum non capax infiniti)*. This was a principle which had appeared during the Christological controversies of the early church, but was to be traced back to rationalistic Greek philosophy. It was this philosophical presupposition which led the Zwinglian group to say that it was impossible for Christ to be present with His body and blood in the Sacrament, since the Ascension had removed Jesus according to His human nature to a faraway realm. For Luther and Melanchthon at Marburg more dangerous even than the sacramental error of the Reformed group was this rationalistic Christology. It was at Marburg that Protestantism was confronted with the fact that two completely different doctrines of Christ had developed.

What has this to do with the present? In the World Council of Churches we are again engaged in discussions on the Lord's Supper. Some participants seem to regard the stand taken by Luther and Melanchthon at Marburg as "sinful." At the same time, there has been what would appear to be an undue optimism on the part of some Lutherans as to the readiness of other Protestants at Oberlin and elsewhere to accept formulations in which

164

are references to the bodily presence of Christ. Zwingli's viewpoint on the Ascension and Christology still stands in the Heidelberg Catechism. And any outward readiness for unity on the part of his spiritual descendants will have no greater significance than did Zwingli's cooperativeness at Marburg, until there is a purging of the rationalistic doctrine that Christ according to His human nature cannot fulfil the promise to be with His followers always. The Lord's Supper cannot be understood or discussed apart from the doctrine of Christ.[10] The reformers offer this important warning for Lutheranism today. Melanchthon expressed it in 1528: "One must draw all theological articles from Christ—how He was born, how He died, how He rose again, etc."[11]

We are now led to the doctrine of justification. It is fashionable today to discuss this doctrine as though it were no more than a matter of taste whether or not one should continue to teach justification by faith. The reformers thought differently. They called this the *Articulus stantis et cadentis ecclesiae*—the article on which the Church will stand or fall. The first generation of Lutherans came from medieval Catholicism. Like Luther, they had experienced the torments of uncertainty about their salvation. They received eagerly the evangelical doctrine of justification. Not since the Apostolic Age had there been such an appreciation for this doctrine, both among teachers and hearers. The vitality of their belief was reflected in the Lutheran Confessions, concluding

---

[10]See the posthumously published book of Werner Elert, *Der Ausgang der altkirchlichen Christologie: Eine Untersuchung über Theodor von Pharan und seine Zeit als Einführung in die alte Dogmengeschichte,* Berlin, 1957.

[11]From the "Unterricht der Visitatorn an die Pfarhern ym Kurfürstenthum zu Sachsen," in Philip Melanchthon, *Werke in Auswahl* [Studienausg.] hrsg. von Robert Stupperich. Gütersloh, 1951, I, 259.

with the Formula of Concord, where justification was defined with symbolical significance.

After Luther, Melanchthon, Bugenhagen, and other leading members of the first generation had died, a partial decline set in. It is true that justification was still genuinely experienced and properly expounded by men as late as Chemnitz, Gerhard and Gerhardt, and Sebastian Bach. Nevertheless a decadence manifested itself in many circles on two points. (1) Justification was sometimes petrified. In a scholastic treatment, the forgiveness of sins and the imputation of Christ's righteousness were split into two successive steps. Thereby the doctrine of imputation lost its significance and came to appear as something unreal, as though God justified men who were not really righteous. This corrupted view of imputation made growth in personal righteousness appear superfluous to many, and led in some cases to false security. (2) Justification was sometimes unduly dramatized. Later followers of Luther were supposed to be able to speak of a religious experience similar to his tower experience. (How absurd it would have seemed to Luther that all others were expected to repeat his experiences as a monk, now that the Gospel had been rediscovered!) Such artificiality demonstrates the tragic fact that the real meaning of justification had been lost. Under the Pietism of Halle there developed the tendency to evoke symptoms of repentance (the *Busskampf*) and the breaking-through of divine grace (the *Gnadendurchbruch*); this emphasis rested especially upon the kind of conversion that August Hermann Francke had had as vicar of St. John Church of Lüneburg. There is a kinship of such a system with the "methods" of Wesleyan Methodism. In Lutheranism, this marked a decline in the people's apprehension of the doctrine of justification.

Our age has inherited this situation. In our congregations, we find, to be sure, many humble believers who have truly experienced justification. On the other hand, just as at the time of Christ or of Luther, we find many self-satisfied Pharisees who trust in themselves that they are righteous, and therefore have little yearning for justification. As observers have noted, justification seems no longer to be interesting to modern men; or, to use the fashionable expression, it seems to have become "irrelevant." A frighteningly subjective word! What if men regarded justification as "irrelevant," while God saw that man really needed to be justified, as He declared in His Word in the days of Jesus and Paul?

Prominent among those who are discussing justification today is Paul Tillich. His book *The Protestant Era* contains weighty criticisms of the Lutheran position. Yet if theologians had expected Tillich to provide a "relevant" substitute when the second volume of his *Systematic Theology* appeared, they were doomed to disappointment. In a discussion limited to less than three pages, Tillich presents a rather dated point of view. He seems unaware of recent discussions among Lutheran dogmaticians and apparently has not himself consulted the sixteenth-century sources. "Justification," he asserts with crushing finality, "is so strange to the modern man that there is scarcely any way of making it intelligible to him."[12]

Let us accept Tillich's assertion as an honest conclusion. But we cannot afford to let his negative judgment silence our concern to preserve this Scriptural article on which the Church stands or falls. While a thorough rebuttal, citing Scripture and history, is manifestly im-

---

[12]Paul Tillich, *The Protestant Era*. 196.

possible within the confines of a brief lecture, let it be
said that from Luther and Melanchthon we can relearn
at least one important truth which makes justification
fully relevant to our day. We learn that men are account-
able before God for every thought, word, and deed.
This covers every area of life, not only what is done on
Sunday, but also what is done, said, and thought Monday through Saturday. Man's responsibility before God
includes such areas as politics, education, race relations,
the international scene, and management and labor problems. The doctrine of justification is internally relevant
to life in the family, community, and church. Justification is not merely a theological category, but a fact in
human experience. Men stand before God the Judge.
And today as yesterday God writes His judgment in huge
letters: "Weighed—and found wanting!"[13]

The chief reason why justification does not seem important to many of our contemporaries seems to be that
they have never grasped the predicament of man in the
presence of God, *coram Deo.* Man must see that justification is his one great need; only then may the all-
embracing relevance of God's favor become clear. Writes
Luther in his last major work, the Commentary on Genesis:

I shall not dispute about the Hebrew word *haschab,*
whether you translate it with *reputare* or *cogitare,* since both
words deal with the same idea. For when the divine majesty
considers me righteous, forgiven of my sins, and set free from
eternal death, by faith I thankfully lay hold on these thoughts
of God concerning me. Thus I am just, not from my works,

---

[13]I should like to direct the reader's attention to Werner Elert's discussion of the *Deus absconditus,* where the God before whom the
sinner is called for an account is portrayed in all His wrath on the
basis of Luther's *De servo arbitrio* of 1525 in his *Morphologie des
Luthertums,* 2. ausg. München, 1952, I, 19. Cf. also the entire discussion
of *Angst,* from Luther through Kierkegaard and Schopenhauer.

but out of faith, by means of which I apprehend God's thoughts.

For God's thought is infallible truth. So when I grasp it, not with uncertainty or doubt, but with steadfast heart, then I am justified.

Faith is a steadfast and certain thought about God or trust in Him, that He is gracious through Christ, and that for Christ's sake He thinks about us thoughts of peace, not thoughts and affliction or wrath.[14]

In today's forum of theological discussion many influential voices cry out against theological controversies. Either out of their conception of Christian love, or else because of intolerance of what they conceive to be intolerance, such voices say that theology can do without debate. It is true that there is no excuse for theological discussions which are carried on in a spirit of animosity. Even during the use of Pietism, however, Philipp Jakob Spener in his *Pia desideria* never suggested that disputations should be abolished, but rather asked that they be held in a spirit of love for one's neighbor. Disputations were an indispensable part of the curriculum at the University of Wittenberg during the Reformation. From the theological faculty they were also brought into other departments such as natural science. Today such areas of learning as medical science and many other fields of a technical kind employ learned debates as one of the better means of testing ideas and learning from others. The fact that there has been little lively discussion in Lutheran theology in America in recent years might be regarded as evidence of a certain theological smugness among us. May it not also mean that there has not been enough life in our theology, and that we have simply been refusing to confront contemporary issues? From Luther and Melanchthon we may learn, in any event, that

---

[14]WA xlii, 563 f.

theological discussion is not an evidence of a lack of brotherly love, but rather an indication that we are concerned about the right interpretation of God's Word.

In American Lutheranism we find ourselves in a minority position. Paramount among the issues which our church is facing is the extent of our participation in what is called the ecumenical movement. We face the future under a tension between loyalty to our confession and the desire to make common cause with other churches. The greatest danger seems to be that we should gradually lose our consciousness of the true nature of Lutheranism. Melanchthon was an example of an individual with an ecumenical outlook. It was his nature to seek for an understanding with the Roman Church on the one side, and the Reformed group on the other. His followers after his death went considerably further than their teacher had gone, and they made dangerous compromises which led not to peace but to controversy. We may learn from them that an alleged love which compromises the truth leads only to strife and weakness. It was only in the Formula of Concord, when the differences between Lutheranism and other faiths were clearly defined, that a way of peaceful co-existence was given. With a sense of history we may learn from past mistakes. And we may learn particularly from Luther to love the truth more than any human forms, including a merely institutional unity. We shall find, I predict, that if Lutheranism has a valuable contribution to give to the ecumenical movement, it will be making that contribution when it adheres faithfully to the teaching of its Confessions which have given it strength and an unequivocal witness to the Word. The nature of that contribution will be a sharing of her insights into a

170

Christocentricity of faith and life, involving in particular the doctrines of the Lord's Supper and of justification.

2. *Improvements Needed in Theological Education*

In spite of the opinions of some of us American Lutherans, it does not appear that strong theological leadership is being exerted in America by the Lutheran Church. Several factors hindered the development of theology in the past. On the one hand, the American frontier, populated by Northern European immigrants, seemed for a long time to require the greater part of the energies and resources of American Lutherans. While our European brethren in their splendid universities were permitted to come to grips with intellectual problems, we were forced into organizational and practical programs. We ought not belittle the great work attempted and accomplished. Nor may we overlook the fact that American Lutheranism has produced some able theologians. Nevertheless the establishing of theological institutions which could compete with the world-renowned universities has had to wait. It is becoming increasingly clear, however, that a constituency of higher intellectual level is now demanding far more than formerly in terms of theological effort. The time is at hand for a renaissance —or may we invent the word naissance?—in Lutheran theology in America. Indeed the movement is already underway, and we may no longer plead lack of funds or men.

What direction should Lutheran theological effort take in the New World? It must grapple with new problems, new opportunities for a responsible and constructive witness, new forms of old heresies. It will not be enough simply to quote other American thinkers from other denominations. Modern problems must be thought out in

171

the frame of reference of our Lutheran heritage. That would indicate a thorough study of our Lutheran Confessions, and together with this, a careful investigation of the theology of Luther, Melanchthon, and other leaders from the past, even as this is being done in Germany, Scandinavia, Holland, and other countries today.

✳ Theological education in America is laboring under a heavy burden: weak pre-theological preparation. Public education in this country has not escaped the baneful results of John Dewey's educational philosophy. A renewal of Lutheran theology cannot be on the basis of a second-hand knowledge of Luther and the Confessions. Thorough training in the Hebrew, Greek, Latin, and German languages is an absolute prerequisite to a vital restatement of the Lutheran witness to the twentieth century. Clearly we need the courage to develop a system in which linguistic, historical, and philosophical knowledge may be acquired. Pre-theological and theological education must go far beyond what is required by accrediting agencies.

It is a notorious fact that many of our public high schools offer little or no training in foreign languages. Unfortunately, even many colleges have not thought it necessary to do this. Could not the academies and junior colleges which have survived some decades of obscurity prepare themselves to contribute splendidly to the present need? It is an important strength of the Missouri Synod that she has never lost sight of the possibilities in this area. The present re-emphasis of the liberal arts in many quarters should be encouraged. Philip Melanchthon would be the first to applaud it! The pre-theological courses are precisely the liberal arts, with language and literature the core of the humanities. Without adequate work in languages, future theologians will lack the skills indispensable to the independent research and fresh results, so vital to any theological rebirth.

Latin and German should by all means be studied in high school. In college, advanced language courses could introduce the students to the theological sources in those tongues. The departments of religion might offer English Bible courses of greater scope and depth than are presently taught, allowing the seminary exegetical departments to work in Hebrew and Greek. The Lutheran liberal arts college could also intensify its efforts to present a unified world-view to future pastors and laymen by giving them a coordinated approach to literature, the visual arts, music and hymnody, architecture, and various branches of philosophy. Likewise the colleges could offer different courses in the life of Luther, the Confessions, and elementary dogmatics, to fit the needs of those not going on to the seminary.

With such a preparation, the student would come to his seminary with a background, including linguistic proficiency, which would enable him to concentrate on theology on a professional level. Instead of remaining with church history, he could go on to study more thoroughly the history of doctrine. He would be prepared to study Luther, Melanchthon, and the Lutheran Symbols from primary sources and to dig far more deeply into the significance of the Lutheran tradition. With such preparation more emphasis could be placed in the seminary upon research and writing. Essays requiring individual initiative might cumulatively prepare the way for future leadership in both pulpit and classroom.

While such a program may seem idealistic, it is not as ambitious as the program our forefathers undertook during the Reformation. At that time, too, the languages had been neglected with evil consequences to the church.

We have only to recall the bitter conflict in which Johann Reuchlin was involved when Johann Pfefferkorn attacked him for his eager espousal of studies in the Hebrew language. Why did Luther welcome Melanchthon so warmly upon his arrival at Wittenberg in 1518? Because a good Greek teacher was urgently needed. Both men found it a worthy life's calling to work for a system in which languages were a part of the theological arsenal of the church. In 1524 Luther wrote an open letter to town councils calling for the establishment of Christian schools. In it he made some remarks which are applicable to today's situation in the United States. He writes:

> For this we cannot deny, that although the Gospel has come to us along through the Holy Ghost, . . . nevertheless it has come by means of languages. In this way it is propagated, and must thereby be preserved. . . . As strongly as we love the Gospel, so strongly let us cleave to the languages. For it was not in vain that God let His Scriptures be written in the two languages. . . .
>
> We shall not be able to keep the Gospel without these languages. The languages are the scabbard in which the sword of the Spirit is concealed. They are the jeweled chest in which this treasure is carried. They are the chalice in which this drink is contained. . . . Yes, if we ever neglect the languages—which God forbid! we shall not only lose the Gospel, but shall finally get to the place where we can no longer correctly read or write Latin or our mother tongue.[15]

Along with a curriculum which provides the tools for research, the church's educational system must provide instruction in methods of research. Teaching loads should be assigned in such a manner that teachers are able to do research of their own and lead their pupils into the joys of exploration in the world of history and of thought.

---

[15]WA xv, 37 f.

3. Some Principles of Research

Not enough attention is given to the methods by which reliable results can be obtained from historical study. We may offer these three principles: 1) Objectivity. 2) Use of primary sources. 3) The critical approach.

What is meant by objectivity? It means that the student approaches his sources with the conviction that they have something to tell him, and that he must be determined to set aside prejudices and preconceived notions. It does not mean, as some have thought, that he is to operate within a vacuum as though he had had no previous knowledge or working hypotheses. When the Lutheran scholar approaches a new area of research, he remains a Lutheran. It is neither necessary nor desirable that he should try to deny the ground on which he stands. Yet he may not allow his previous experience to influence his investigation in such a way that the evidence is distorted by essentially dishonest selectivity.

Next, use the primary sources. In his famous inaugural address at Wittenberg in 1518, Melanchthon began a career in the course of which the entire German educational system was significantly changed. He announced this basic principle: back to the sources! It has been pointed out that modern scientific method goes back to Melanchthon's work as the educator of Germany, *Praeceptor Germaniae*. There can be little question that the methodology of natural science is built upon this same principle of examination of primary data, and Melanchthon is in part responsible. The same stringent methodology is necessary in theological science. Some may be surprised to hear theology called a science. But theology deals with data which, while not objective in the same sense, are even more important than those of the natural scientist. Should not the theologian study the Word of God, the history of the Church, her historical symbols, or her practical problems, with the same careful attention that the chemist or physicist devotes to natural phenomena?

This is especially necessary in church history or in Luther research. The original sources alone are authoritative, not a book which someone has written, be it ever so helpful. Not what Holl or Elert or Hirsch or a dozen other fine scholars may have written about Luther, but the words of Luther himself are the authority.

With which primary sources should one begin his study of the Reformation? First, the Lutheran Confessions as found in the *Book of Concord* should be carefully studied by the candidate for the Lutheran ministry—the more so since he pledges himself to teach in accord with these Symbols! The chief work of Melanchthon after this would be the *Loci communes*, especially in the edition of 1521. His polemic against Rhadinus (1521) and his "Instruction to the Visitors of the Saxon Churches" (1528) should also stand high on the list. Every serious student of Lutheran theology ought to purchase the new *Studienausgabe* of Melanchthon's works.

As to which writings of Luther to read first, the problem is greater because of the tremendous choice available. The beginner will not go wrong in starting with Luther's sermons and other devotional writings like the *Magnificat.* The busy pastor, particularly, can gain many a refreshing insight through such a delightful study. Nevertheless Luther's more distinctly theological treatises should not be neglected. In keeping with our general theme of the mature Luther, I should suggest starting with the Lectures on Galatians of the 1530's, followed by the *Grosse Bekenntnis das Heiligen Sakraments* of 1528. A thorough study of his *De servo arbitrio* of 1525

176

is also indispensable. Nor may one overlook the young Luther. His Lectures on Romans would be the background for an investigation of his earlier years, and the 1519 commentary on Galatians is an important source for his transitional years. Of great importance also are the three reform treatises of 1520 and the "Treatise on Good Works." Beyond these, the Weimar Edition, or the fine new American Edition, places almost no limits upon the pastor-scholar.

We have mentioned two rules for reaching dependable conclusions in research. The first was to be objective, and the second was to use the source material, rather than depending on the findings and judgments of secondary literature. The third rule is to approach the sources critically. In dealing with Luther, for example, we must first ask: What was the historical setting of the work under consideration? If it was written for devotional purposes, we must not expect fine theological distinctions from it. If we are reading from one of Luther's disputations, we must be extremely careful to see that we are quoting Luther and not his opponent, or that Luther is not pressing his point to best his opponent. If we are dealing with one of Luther's great polemical treatises, we shall have to ask such questions as these: What was the nature of the error that Luther was trying to overcome? Who was his opponent? Was Luther using irony? We might even have to ask: Has Luther correctly understood the point of view of the other man? If we are reading Luther's sermons, we must be particularly concerned about their authenticity. Has a particular group of sermons come down through a dependable transcriber like Rorer, or do they stem from the pen of a man like Roth, who did considerable editing in preparing them for publication? A special warning is needed to interpret the Table Talk with caution. These casual utterances of Luther are not to be pressed for academic distinctions. Ordinarily they are used only as corroborative evidence, after a given teaching has been established in writings of unquestioned authenticity. Regardless of what work we are studying, we must always ask: At what point in Luther's life did he make this statement? Was it made by the young Luther, by the Luther in transition, or by the reformer in his old age? What theological, historical, and contemporary conditions influenced the statement? Does it have permanent standing in Luther's thinking, or did he later abandon it? And these are only a few of the questions that the investigator must bear in mind as he approaches his historical subject.

And now we must conclude with the question with which we began. Does Martin Luther have a message for the Church today? I trust that this hour has revealed that although this great father of our church has been dead for more than four centuries, he can still speak out with a certainty and a clarity which are of great help even to us of the twentieth century. To our church is given the task of making known his witness to evangelical truth to other groups in the *oikoumene*. May God help her to overcome the problems that stand in the way. May God make fruitful the renaissance that is now beginning to appear in American Lutheran theology. Our goal must be: Every pastor a competent theologian. Our program must be to have a ministerium composed of a group of theologians who read and know Luther and Melanchthon. Mere repetitions of their names or superficial use of characteristic Lutheran terms as shibboleths will be fruitless. Their significance consists in the fact that they became instruments in God's hand through whom the Gospel was revealed to their own age. Therefore we must know them. God has used them in our own lifetime to lead the Lutheran Churches in Europe back to the Gospel. May Luther and Melanchthon also in America be allowed their contribution toward a renaissance in our theology!